PRACTICE
MAKES
PERFECT

# Intermediate English Grammar for ESL Learners

## Second Edition

**Robin Torres-Gouzerh**

McGraw Hill Education

New York   Chicago   San Francisco   Athens   London   Madrid
Mexico City   Milan   New Delhi   Singapore   Sydney   Toronto

1 2 3 4 5 6 7 8 9 10   RHR/RHR   1 2 1 0 9 8 7 6 5

ISBN        978-0-07-184051-4
MHID        0-07-184051-6

Ebook ISBN  978-0-07-177169-6
MHID        0-07-177169-7


Interior design by Village Typographers, Inc.

Trademarks: McGraw-Hill Education, the McGraw-Hill Education Publishing logo, Practice Makes Perfect, and related trade dress are trademarks or registered trademarks of McGraw-Hill Education and/or its affiliates in the United States and other countries and may not be used without written permission. All other trademarks are the property of their respective owners. McGraw-Hill Education is not associated with any product or vendor mentioned in this book.

McGraw-Hill Education books are available at special quantity discounts to use as premiums and sales promotions or for use in corporate training programs. To contact a representative, please visit the Contact Us pages at www.mhprofessional.com.

---

**Extra Exercise Questions**

Additional review exercises that support this book can be found in the McGraw-Hill Education Language Lab App. Go to www.mhlanguagelab.com for details on how to access this free app, which is available for Apple and Android tablet and mobile devices, as well as for computer via web browser.

# Contents

# Preface

Grammar can be frustrating to master as you try to learn a language. This book was written to be easily accessible to students of English as a second language. *Practice Makes Perfect: Intermediate English Grammar for ESL Learners* is designed to help beginner- and intermediate-level learners hone their grammatical skills to the point where they are comfortable with English grammar. Technical terminology has been kept to a minimum, and simple terms are used wherever possible. As a result, you will be able to focus on learning new material.

You have already begun your study of English grammar. This book will provide you with a higher-level look at that grammar. The numerous examples provide models on which you can rely to form your own original sentences. The many practical exercises give you the opportunity to practice what you have learned. Be sure to use the answer key to check your work. And this second edition is supported by additional review questions in the McGraw-Hill Education Language Lab app.

As you progress through this book, you will find that your confidence in using English is growing, and by the time you finish the book, you will be one major step closer to being a fluent speaker and writer.

# The sentence

In formal spoken or written English, every sentence must be **complete**. The basic rule is that all sentences must have a **subject** (S), which can be a **pronoun**, a **noun**, or a **noun phrase**, and a **verb** (V), which can also be a **verb phrase**. In many cases, the verb can be followed by a **direct object** (O). Consider the following examples.

> She works.  (S) + (V)
> Fish swim.  (S) + (V)
> The children played.  (S) + (V)
> The bus driver needs a break.  (S) + (V) + (O)
> My mother liked the movie.  (S) + (V) + (O)

Every sentence must have a **subject**. The imperative sentence is an exception to this basic rule, because the subject, *you*, is understood. Imperative sentences are used to instruct someone to do something.

> **Go** to class.
> **Pick up** your mess, please.
> **Read** objective newspapers.

Verbs that do not require a direct object are called **intransitive verbs**. Some common intransitive verbs are *exist* and *rise*. They are typically used with prepositional phrases, as illustrated in the following examples.

> It is possible that life **existed** on Mars millions of years ago.
> Black smoke **rose** from the burning tires.

---

**EXERCISE**

## 1·1

*Rewrite each verb phrase as a complete sentence by adding a subject.*

EXAMPLE   Is a real bargain. ___*That coat is a real bargain.*___

1. Were eating an Italian specialty.

   _____

2. Have worked in Austin for two years.

   _____

3. Purchased it last week. _____

4. Is awful. _____

5. Looks comfortable. _____

6. Went to the theater. _____

# Noun phrases

The subject of a sentence can be a **noun phrase**, which can be **simple** or **complex**. The subject can be one word or a group of words that includes a noun together with other words that provide information about the noun. Some noun phrases can be quite complex. Consider the following sentences.

> **The boy** went to the playground.
> **The lively boy** went to the playground.
> **The lively boy next door** went to the playground.

No matter how complex a noun phrase is, it still remains the subject of the sentence and determines the form of the verb. The verb in the sentences above is *went*.

*Underline the subject(s) in each sentence.*

1. Children ought to be more careful.

2. Water is good for you.

3. Prague is an amazing and historic Eastern European city.

4. The furry, clean, calm cat slept on the couch.

5. The furry, clean, calm, black cat ran outside.

6. The furry, clean, calm, black cat with a scar jumped on the counter.

7. The big, ugly, dirty, brown bear with long ears and large claws attacked a hunter.

8. She read a magazine yesterday.

9. Peter went to the circus.

10. Lending money and giving too much advice can cause problems.

# Verb phrases

The verb in a sentence can also appear in a **verb phrase**.

> He **has** often **spoken** of you.
> She **will** not **be able** to understand this document.

Sometimes extra information is added before the subject and verb, or between the subject and the verb. This information is often adverbial. In the first example below, the adverbial phrases tell **where**, **how frequently**, and **when** the action took place. In the second example, the adverbial phrase tells **why** and **when** the action took place.

> **In Pennsylvania**, Marc **often** went running **in the morning**.
> Marc, **because he was feeling unhealthy**, went running **in the morning**.

In both of these examples, when we ask the question "Who went running?" the answer is "Marc"—the subject of both sentences. The added information is that he often ran in the morning when he was in Pennsylvania, and that he ran because he felt unhealthy.

EXERCISE
1·3

*Underline both the subject and the verb or verb phrase in each sentence.*

1. The big, brown dog sitting in the shade is hungry.

2. I always drink coffee in the morning before work.

3. After getting to the hotel room, Saul ordered room service.

4. The youth hostels we stayed in while we were in Budapest weren't too expensive.

5. My professor, after noticing that I had been studying hard, was nicer to me.

6. Maybe her father is sicker than you think.

7. In the future, presidential elections will be held on the Internet.

8. After the show, the people who were sitting in the front row got up.

# Modifiers

There are many types of sentence modifiers. Among the most important are **adjectives**, **adverbs**, and **prepositional phrases**.

Adjectives modify nouns or pronouns.

> That **striped** snake is poisonous.
> Our **new** neighbor is a **professional** basketball player.
> He is **old**.

Adverbs modify verbs, adjectives, or other adverbs.

> She **seldom** wrote after she moved away.
> The **severely** wounded man was taken to the hospital.
> The witness spoke **very** nervously about the robbery.

Prepositional phrases can modify nouns or verbs.

> The man **in the garden** is a police officer.
> **For many years** they lived **in Mexico**.

Complete each sentence with an appropriate modifier: adjective, adverb, or prepositional phrase.

EXAMPLE     They stayed up and chatted ___until dawn___.

1. _____ he headed for home on foot.

2. Do you recognize the _____ man on the corner?

3. She _____ speaks to me anymore.

4. _____ I was at Macy's hoping to buy a _____ dress.

5. He took her advice very _____.

6. _____, we _____ go skiing in Colorado.

7. Your _____ brother plays the piano _____.

8. Please speak _____. I'm trying to nap.

9. Yesterday, I saw a _____ accident _____.

10. My sister is a _____ competent lawyer.

# The verb phrase

It is impossible to compose a correct sentence without using a proper verb. The verb is at the very foundation of a sentence. The **verb phrase** may be composed of only one word or it may have related parts. Consider the following examples.

> Angela **had to go** to Chicago.
> The boys **are fishing** at the creek.
> Someone **should repair** that window.

Sometimes, the related parts are composed of more than one word. In the examples above, the verbs are *go, fish,* and *repair,* and the related parts are *had to, are,* and *should.*

EXERCISE

## 2·1

*Underline the verb phrase in each sentence, whether the verb phrase is composed of a verb alone or a verb and related parts.*

1. He doesn't go to meetings on Tuesdays.

2. He goes to the park with his dog.

3. She is heading out to school.

4. He never washes the dishes.

5. She is going to the theater tonight.

6. He has traveled to Spain before.

7. She has been practicing yoga for two years now.

8. He has to be at the train station by 8 A.M.

9. She goes to school in Chicago.

10. She had visited Chicago many times.

11. She is going to travel to Chicago.

# Auxiliary verbs

Some sentences contain a single verb (for example, *go*), while other sentences include a related part before the main verb (for example, a form of *be* + a form of the verb *go*). **Auxiliary verbs** are among the related parts that can form a verb phrase; in some grammar books, they are called "helping verbs." The second example below illustrates the verb *be* used as an auxiliary.

> She goes to class.
> She **is going** to class.

The first sentence contains a form of the single verb *go*. In the second example, however, the sentence also contains the verb *go*, but this time it has a related part, the auxiliary verb *is*, which precedes the verb in its present participle form (*is going*).

Auxiliary verbs change how a verb is used. Such changes can affect the tense, mood, or even the meaning of the verb.

The auxiliary *be* can be used in any tense, and in every tense the main verb is in the form of a present participle.

| | |
|---|---|
| PRESENT | She **is fixing** that old clock. |
| PAST | She **was fixing** that old clock. |
| PRESENT PERFECT | She **has been fixing** that old clock. |
| PAST PERFECT | She **had been fixing** that old clock. |
| FUTURE | She **will be fixing** that old clock. |

The auxiliary verb *have* is used with a past participle to form the present perfect or past perfect tense.

> She **has lived** here all her life.
> They **have been working** on the problem all day.
> Martin **had** never **seen** a kangaroo before.
> She **had been napping** when the fire broke out.

The auxiliary *do/did* is used with a basic verb to form a **question**, a **negative statement** with *not,* or an **emphatic statement**. *Do* is used in the present tense, and *did* in the past tense.

> **Do** you **understand** Arabic?
> **Did** Mr. Keller **sell** that old car yet?
> You **don't have** enough money to buy that CD.
> You're wrong. I **do have** enough money.
> But you **did not have** enough money yesterday.

# Modal auxiliaries

Some auxiliary verbs are called **modal auxiliaries**. They are used with a verb to show the **degree of obligation** of the action of the verb. Two important modal auxiliaries are *have to* and *should*.

> **Do** you **have to play** the radio so loud?
> Mary **has to stay** at home today.
> Dad, you **should**n't **work** so hard in this heat.
> Why **should** I **care**?

*Underline the auxiliary verb in each sentence.*

1. He **does** attend meetings on Tuesdays.

2. He **is** walking to the park with his dog.

3. She **is** leaving for summer camp on Sunday.

4. Alberto **has** gone to Cuba.

5. He **has** traveled to the south of Spain for years.

6. She **should** go alone this time.

7. He **has** to walk faster.

*Rewrite each sentence three times: (1) with* be *and a present participle,
(2) in the present perfect tense, and (3) with the modal auxiliary* should.

EXAMPLE        They speak with a lawyer.

   *They are speaking with a lawyer.*

   *They have spoken with a lawyer.*

   *They should speak with a lawyer.*

1. James tries on a pair of pants.

   _____

   _____

   _____

2. I live on about a hundred dollars a week.

   _____

   _____

   _____

3. Father scolds the children.

   _____

   _____

   _____

4. Does she work hard?

   _____

   _____

5. The conductor waits on the platform.

   _____

   _____

   _____

# The verb

Verbs are words that express action. They can express **tense** (the time at which the action occurred) and **voice**. The voice can be **active** (where the subject performs the action) or **passive** (where the subject is placed in a passive position in the sentence).

The most common verb tenses are the **present**, **past**, and **future**. Each of these tenses has a **progressive**, **habitual**, and **perfect** form.

## Linking verbs

A linking verb connects a subject and a subject complement, a word that describes or clarifies the subject. The most commonly used linking verb is the verb *be*. Consider the following examples.

> Table tennis **is** fun.
> Their grandfather **was** a war hero.

Other words commonly used as linking verbs are *appear, seem, look, feel, sound, taste*, and *smell*.

> You **seem** a little unhappy today.
> That woman **looks** rather sick.
> This sweater **feels** warm.
> Her meatloaf **smells** great!

Linking verbs are intransitive. They do not have direct objects. Notice that the verb in each of the following examples is a transitive verb with the direct object *flower*.

> The little girl **smelled** the flower.
> No one wanted to **buy** a flower from her.
> I only **sold** one flower today.

To identify the direct object in a sentence, ask *what* or *whom* of the verb: **What** *did the little girl smell?* **What** *did no one want to buy?* **What** *did I sell today?* The answer to each question is *flower,* the direct object. Linking verbs never have a direct object.

*Complete each sentence with an appropriate linking verb.*

1. Her suggestion _____ useful at the time.

2. Barbara _____ very different with her new haircut.

3. From here, clouds _____ fluffy like cotton balls.

4. Chocolate éclairs _____ my favorite pastry.

5. This honey _____ wonderful.

6. That idea _____ crazy to them.

7. Peter told me he _____ sick today.

Most verbs have five forms:

* **Base form.** This is the verb in its original form, the form you find in the dictionary. *Run, study, eat, think, write, fall, open,* and *ask* are verbs in their base form.

* **Third-person singular form: base form + -s (or -es).** This form is used with *he, she,* or *it* in the present tense. *Runs, studies, eats, thinks, writes, falls, opens,* and *asks* are verbs in the third-person singular form.

* **Past tense form.** This form can be regular or irregular. The regular past tense is the base form + *-ed. Studied, opened,* and *asked* are verbs in the regular past tense form. There are fewer irregular verbs in the English language than regular verbs. These verbs are called **irregular**, because they do not end with *-ed* in the past tense. *Ran, ate, thought, wrote,* and *fell* are past tense forms of irregular verbs.

* **Present participle, or progressive, form: base form + -ing.** *Running, studying, eating, thinking, writing, falling, opening,* and *asking* are verbs in the present participle, or progressive, form.

* **Past participle form.** This form can be regular or irregular. The regular past participle form is the base form + *-ed. Studied, opened,* and *asked* are verbs in this form. Irregular past participles are formed differently, for example, *run, eaten, thought, written,* and *fallen.*

# Irregular verbs

Verbs are categorized as irregular when they do not end in *-ed* in the past tense form. Although there are fewer irregular verbs than regular verbs, they are also among the most commonly used verbs.

The following chart illustrates the various forms of some common irregular verbs. This list is not comprehensive; a complete list can be found in most dictionaries.

| BASE FORM | THIRD-PERSON SINGULAR | PAST TENSE | PRESENT PARTICIPLE | PAST PARTICIPLE |
|---|---|---|---|---|
| cut | cuts | cut | cutting | cut |
| eat | eats | ate | eating | eaten |
| find | finds | found | finding | found |
| go | goes | went | going | gone |
| run | runs | ran | running | run |
| say | says | said | saying | said |
| speak | speaks | spoke | speaking | spoken |
| think | thinks | thought | thinking | thought |
| write | writes | wrote | writing | written |

The verb *be* is an exception. Like other verbs, it has a base form (*be*), a progressive form (*being*), and a past participle (*been*). Yet the present tense of *be* has three distinct forms: (I) *am*, (he/she/it) *is*, and (we/you/they) *are*. Moreover, the past tense of *be* has two distinct forms: (I/he/she/it) *was* and (we/you/they) *were*.

# Tenses

Most verbs can be conjugated in the present, past, and future tenses. The present participle, or progressive form, of a verb is used together with the auxiliary *be* to show a **continuing** or **incomplete action** in the various tenses. Consider the verb *speak* in its progressive form.

| | |
|---|---|
| PRESENT | She **is speaking** with John. |
| PAST | She **was speaking** with John. |
| PRESENT PERFECT | She **has been speaking** with John. |
| PAST PERFECT | She **had been speaking** with John. |
| FUTURE | She **will be speaking** with John. |
| FUTURE PERFECT | She **will have been speaking** with John. |

Compare these sentences with the following sentences, which illustrate a **completed** or **habitual action**.

| | |
|---|---|
| PRESENT | She **speaks** with John. |
| PAST | She **spoke** with John. |
| PRESENT PERFECT | She **has spoken** with John. |
| PAST PERFECT | She **had spoken** with John. |
| FUTURE | She **will speak** with John. |
| FUTURE PERFECT | She **will have spoken** with John. |

The progressive form of *be* (*being*) is used only in the present and past tenses.

| | | |
|---|---|---|
| PRESENT | He is sick. | He **is being** good. |
| PAST | He was sick. | He **was being** good. |
| PRESENT PERFECT | He has been sick. | — |
| PAST PERFECT | He had been sick. | — |
| FUTURE | He will be sick. | — |
| FUTURE PERFECT | He will have been sick. | — |

*Rewrite each present-tense sentence using the other five tenses.*

1. I study mathematics.

   PAST                  _____

   PRESENT PERFECT       _____

   PAST PERFECT          _____

   FUTURE                _____

   FUTURE PERFECT        _____

2. Tom is going to Iraq.

   PAST                  _____

   PRESENT PERFECT       _____

   PAST PERFECT          _____

   FUTURE                _____

   FUTURE PERFECT        _____

3. Anna comes along.

   PAST                  _____

   PRESENT PERFECT       _____

   PAST PERFECT          _____

   FUTURE                _____

   FUTURE PERFECT        _____

4. They are driving to Arizona.

   PAST                  _____

   PRESENT PERFECT       _____

   PAST PERFECT          _____

   FUTURE                _____

   FUTURE PERFECT        _____

*In each sentence, if the verb illustrates habitual action, rewrite the sentence with the progressive form of the verb. If the verb is the progressive form, rewrite the sentence to illustrate habitual action. Retain the tense of the original sentence.*

1. Why is he running so fast?

   _____

2. The boys swam across the river.

   _____

3. The hungry campers have eaten the hot dogs.

   _____

4. I won't be going to work today.

   _____

5. The old woman was very nice to me.

   _____

6. My uncle has sung in a chorus.

   _____

7. Will you drive your dad's new car?

   _____

8. I was thinking about you.

   _____

9. We had shopped there.

   _____

10. We were camping on the side of a hill.

   _____

# The progressive tenses

Most verbs can form a present participle and be used in the progressive tenses. These tenses express the idea that an action is in progress during a particular time, that an action begins before, is in progress during, and continues after a period of time or after another action begins.

## The present progressive

The present progressive tense expresses an action that is taking place at the moment of speaking and can imply that the action is incomplete.

Lauren **is shopping** right now. (INCOMPLETE ACTION: *She is still shopping.*)
He **is traveling** to Germany. (INCOMPLETE ACTION: *He hasn't arrived yet.*)
The sun **is shining** brightly. (INCOMPLETE ACTION: *The sun continues to shine.*)
The girls **are walking** to the park. (INCOMPLETE ACTION: *They haven't arrived yet.*)

Often, the progressive present tense can be used to imply a future tense meaning.

I **am driving** home this weekend.
**Are** you **going** to college next fall?

## The past progressive

The past progressive tense expresses an action that took place in the past but was in progress for a period of time or was incomplete.

Lauren **was shopping** all day. (IN PROGRESS ALL DAY)
The boys **were fighting** over a toy. (IN PROGRESS FOR A PERIOD OF TIME)
Tim **was studying** but got tired and took a nap. (INCOMPLETE)
They **were driving** home when they ran out of gas. (INCOMPLETE)

It is quite common to add a *when* clause to statements that show an incomplete action or an action in progress that is interrupted.

She was crying **when** I arrived.
Mom was trying to rest **when** the phone rang.
We were just sitting down to supper **when** our neighbor knocked at the door.
Mary was practicing the piano **when** I dropped by.

*Complete each sentence with an appropriate* when *clause.*

EXAMPLE    She was just getting out of bed when ___*the doorbell rang*___ .

1. I was leaning back in my chair when _____ .

2. Were you standing on the corner when _____?

3. Aunt Doris was baking a cake when _____ .

4. We were making up the bed in the spare room when _____

_____ .

*Now, provide an appropriate progressive-tense clause to complete each sentence.*

EXAMPLE    ___*I was just opening my eyes*___ when I heard Mom come in.

5. _____ when the dog began to bark.

6. _____ when the door slammed shut.

7. _____ when I heard someone call my name.

8. _____ when the road suddenly ended.

9. _____ when a bee stung me.

10. _____ when someone stole my purse.

It is possible to place a past progressive verb in a clause that begins with *while* in order to emphasize that the action was in progress when an interruption occurred.

**While** I was swimming in the pool, I felt sick.
My brother began to cry **while** I was trying to study.
**While** you were out jogging, someone broke into the house.
**While** he was standing at the bus stop, it started to snow.

A *when* clause and a *while* clause can be used with the same sentence elements.

**While** he was standing at the bus stop, it started to snow.
He was standing at the bus stop **when** it started to snow.

**While** Father was working in the basement, I fell and broke my arm.
Father was working in the basement **when** I fell and broke my arm.

The interruption of an action in progress can be another action in progress.

While I **was trying** to fall asleep in my apartment, the upstairs neighbor **was making** noise.
She **was checking** the test results while I **was working** in the lab.

*Change each sentence from a statement containing a* when *clause to a statement containing a* while *clause.*

1. They were opening their Christmas gifts when the Christmas tree fell over.

   _____

   _____

2. Tom was swimming in the pool when his little brother fell in the water.

   _____

   _____

3. She was speaking with the letter carrier when a taxi pulled up in front of the house.

   _____

   _____

4. Ms. Howard was lecturing her class when her cell phone rang.

   _____

   _____

5. The boys were playing checkers on the floor when the cat jumped into the middle of their game.

   _____

   _____

# The future progressive

The future progressive tense expresses an action in progress or incomplete that will be taking place at a time in the future.

> Lauren **will be shopping** when I call her.
> We **will be traveling** by car.
> **Will** you **be having** dinner with us tonight?
> The two boys **will be sharing** a room together.

As with the present and past progressive tenses, the future progressive is used to express an action in progress that is interrupted.

> He **will be cooking** when we get there.
> The children **will** probably **be sleeping** when you peek in on them.
> When you open your eyes, you **will be standing** in your new house.
> **Will** you still **be working** in the garden when I stop by?

Note that, although the clause with the progressive form of the verb is in the future tense, the verb in the *when* clause is in the present tense.

She **will be preparing** breakfast when the flowers **arrive**.

This difference of tenses also occurs with *while* clauses: The *while* clause is in the present tense, and the main clause is in the future tense.

While you're out skiing, **I'll be making** some lunch.

In some cases, the simple future and the future progressive tenses express very similar situations or actions, especially when the future action takes place at an indefinite time in the future. In the following examples, note that both sentences express an almost identical situation: We can't say for sure at what time Tyler is coming, but he is expected soon.

Tyler **will come** soon.
Tyler **will be coming** soon.

EXERCISE
4·3

*Complete each sentence, using either the simple present or the present progressive tense of the verb in parentheses.*

EXAMPLE     Cecilia can't come to the door because she ___is washing___ (wash) her hair.

1. David _____ (wash) his car every weekend.

2. Paul usually _____ (eat) in front of the building, but today he

   _____ (eat) at the far corner table.

3. Please explain it to me again. I _____ (try) to understand your explanation.

4. I sent Paul an e-mail last week, but I haven't received an answer yet.

   I _____ (still + wait) for his reply.

5. I was getting tired of gray skies. I'm glad the sun _____ (shine) again this morning.

6. Every morning at ten, the heater _____ (turn on) and

   _____ (stay on) until mid-afternoon.

7. It's so cold! No wonder it _____ (hail).

8. Tyler is a basketball player, but he _____ (not + play) right now, because it's off-season.

9. He _____ (coach) kids during the summer, and he

   _____ (train) in the fall.

10. In the spring, he _____ (attend) school in the morning and

    _____ (play) with his team in the afternoon.

*Complete each sentence, using either the simple past or the past progressive tense of the verb in parentheses.*

EXAMPLE   I ____went____ (go) to the park last week, but it ___was not___ (not + be) sunny at all.

1. I _____ (call) Kim yesterday morning, but she

   _____ (not + be) at home. She _____ (visit)

   her aunt like she usually does on Tuesday mornings.

2. I _____ (hear) the neighbors washing their dishes last night,

   because I _____ (be) awake.

3. The weather was perfect yesterday when we had the picnic at Peace Park.

   The sun _____ (shine). A rather pleasant wind

   _____ (blow). The children _____ (run) around

   all day.

4. My parents _____ (joke) about something when

   I _____ (enter) the room. They instantly

   _____ (stop) and _____ (pretend)

   they _____ (do) something else.

5. I received a package from Korea in the mail. When I _____ (open) it,

   I _____ (find) a letter from my girlfriend and a couple of pictures.

6. While Pedro _____ (organize) his jazz records, his sister Miranda

   _____ (dust) off the turntables.

7. Steven _____ (prefer) the science fiction stories he heard on the radio.

8. While his dad _____ (tell) him the story of the Three Mosquitoes, Steven

   _____ (fall) asleep, so his dad quietly _____ (close)

   the book and silently _____ (walk) out of the room.

9. Mike _____ (run) down the stairs when his foot

   _____ (catch) in one of the rails. Unfortunately,

   he _____ (break) his knee and ankle.

*Complete each sentence, using either the present progressive or the future progressive tense of the verb in parentheses.*

EXAMPLE     Right now, I am playing. Tomorrow at this time, I ___*will be working*___ (work).

1. I will leave the university at three tomorrow. When I _____ (arrive) at yoga class, my friends _____ (wait) for me to begin the warm-up exercises.

2. ARCHIE: When do you leave for summer camp?

   VANESSA: In a couple of days. Can you believe it? A week from now,

   I _____ (sleep) under the stars. I _____ (climb) mountains.

   ARCHIE: Sounds like fun! I _____ (think) of you the whole time.

3. ALFONSO: Are you going to be downtown next Saturday evening?

   CATHERINE: No, I don't think so. I _____ (stay) home to finish painting my living room.

4. Look at those dark clouds on the horizon. I bet by the time our drive

   _____ (be) over and we get home, it _____ (rain).

5. Next winter at this time, I _____ (use) the exact same gloves I am using right now. They're just way too expensive.

6. RICHARD: How will I reach you if your cell-phone battery goes dead?

   MICHAEL: I _____ (stay) at the Thunderbird and

   I _____ (be) pretty sure they have phones in the rooms.

# The perfect tenses

The perfect tenses are formed with the auxiliary verb *have* + a past participle. The perfect tenses express the idea that an action was begun in the past and continued until a later time.

## The present perfect

The present perfect tense is so named because the auxiliary *have* is conjugated in the present tense. It is used to describe an action that began in the past and continues until the present.

> She **has drawn** her mom a picture every day for the past two weeks.
> I **haven't met** anyone interesting since I moved into this apartment complex.
> I **have navigated** a sailboat many times.
> He **has** already **showered**.

When combined with prepositional phrases that start with *since* or *for*, the present perfect can also express an action or situation that began in the past and that is still taking place in the present. Note that the concept of an action in progress or incomplete is expressed in the present perfect by a verb formed in the progressive.

> I **have had** these red gloves for three years.
> I **have liked** *Harold and the Purple Crayon* since I was five years old.
> I **have been living** on this island for two years.
> I **have been standing** here since eight o'clock.

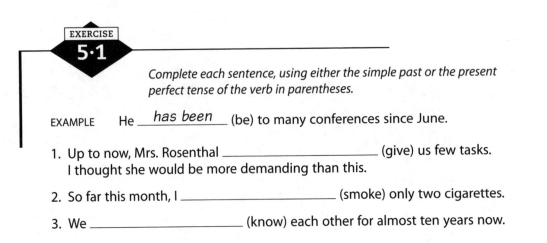

**EXERCISE**

**5·1**

*Complete each sentence, using either the simple past or the present perfect tense of the verb in parentheses.*

EXAMPLE    He ___has been___ (be) to many conferences since June.

1. Up to now, Mrs. Rosenthal _____ (give) us few tasks. I thought she would be more demanding than this.

2. So far this month, I _____ (smoke) only two cigarettes.

3. We _____ (know) each other for almost ten years now.

4. In my whole lifetime, I _____ (never + see) such a violent storm.

5. Last November, I _____ (feel) heartbroken for the first time in my life.

6. Try not to talk too loudly again before the end of the movie.

You _____ (already + annoy) the people sitting behind us.

You _____ (get) us in trouble the last time we came to this theater.

7. Henry _____ (be) here since the Easter holidays.

8. Olivia _____ (land) in Hawaii four hours ago.

9. Alicia _____ (break) the door last weekend, but it was an accident.

EXERCISE

5·2

*Practice forming past participles by beginning each sentence with* I have never + *the past participle of the verb in parentheses.*

EXAMPLE ___*I have never left*___ (leave) my shoes in a restaurant.

1. _____ (feed) a tiger.

2. _____ (read) *Lord of the Flies.*

3. _____ (wreck) my car.

4. _____ (understand) Albert Einstein's theory of relativity.

5. _____ (think) about Darwin's theory of evolution.

6. _____ (build) a house.

7. _____ (fly) a kite.

8. _____ (hold) a baby.

9. _____ (sleep) in a tent.

10. _____ (travel) to Russia.

11. _____ (teach) English.

12. _____ (vote) for local representatives.

13. _____ (listen) to Charles Mingus.

14. _____ (catch) a butterfly.

15. _____ (make) a blueberry pie.

16. _____ (win) the lottery.

17. _____ (send) an e-mail to the chief of staff of the U.S. Army.

18. _____ (eat) chicken ice cream.

19. _____ (steal) a bike.

20. _____ (fall) off a cliff.

21. _____ (bring) a penguin to class.

22. _____ (forget) my name.

23. _____ (drink) absinth.

# Chronological references

Certain references to time require the use of a specific tense. The present perfect tense is used when the chronological reference is to an action begun in the past and continuing into the present. The simple past tense indicates that the action was completed in the past. Following are examples of chronological references that suggest the use of the present perfect tense.

> I have worked here **since the beginning of November**.
> Have you lived here **for a long time**?
> **During the past year**, Pedro has seen several accidents at this corner.

The progressive form of the present perfect can be used to emphasize that an action is in progress or continues over a long period of time.

> **In the last few weeks**, we have been traveling over much of Europe.

Compare these chronological references with ones that suggest the use of the simple past tense.

> Helena bought several new blouses **yesterday**.
> Were you in Boston again **last week**?
> She stayed in the old house for only a few days **after her grandmother died**.
> Bill lost over a hundred dollars **while in Las Vegas**.

## EXERCISE
### 5·3

*Complete each sentence with appropriate chronological references. Use any reference you wish (for example, dates, days, or years), as long as it makes sense in the sentence.*

EXAMPLES  Today is ___the 12th of January___. I first met my English teacher ___five months ago___. I have known him since ___September___.
I have known him for ___five months___.

Today is ___Monday___. I first met my English teacher ___last week___. I have known him since ___Tuesday___. I have known him for ___six days___.

1. Today is _____. I bought this book _____.

   I have had this book since _____. I have had it for

   _____.

2. I first decided she was my best friend _____. I have known her

   for _____. I have known her since _____.

3. It is 200_____. I started going to school in 19_____/200_____. I have been a student for

   _____. I have been a student since _____.

4. Yesterday was _____. I moved to this town

   _____. I have been living in this town since

   _____. I have been here for _____.

EXERCISE
5·4

Complete each sentence, using either the simple past or the present perfect tense of the verb in parentheses.

EXAMPLE   What ___has she bought___ (she + buy) since she ___walked in___ (walk in)
          the store?

1. Since the end of the nineteenth century, scientists _____ (make)
   many important discoveries.

2. Thanks to new techniques and new discoveries, medical analysis

   _____ (advance) a great deal in the twentieth century.

3. Economic systems are different from those implemented in the 1800s. For example,

   the information gathered to conduct analysis _____ (change)

   greatly through the years. In the 1800s, these systems _____ (be)

   mainly focused on national indicators. Today, however, international economies

   _____ (become) efficient, and it is necessary to take them

   into account. In the 1800s, domestic economies _____ (be)

   self-sufficient and could survive with little trade. Today, all economies, small and large,

   are connected.

4. It's undeniable that she _____ (get) older since we last saw her,

   but one can't deny she _____ (also + get) wiser. She also seems

   to _____ (become) funnier.

5. Yesterday, my father and I _____ (have) some free time,

   so we _____ (go) to watch the movie *Hotel Rwanda*. We then

   headed out to a coffeehouse and _____ (talk) about it for

   hours.

6. What _____ (you + learn) since you

_____ (begin) reading this chapter?

7. How many people _____ (you + meet) who only spoke English?

I hope you _____ (already + meet) many interesting people.

8. PAUL: Do you like beef jerky?

LAURA: I don't know, I _____ (never + taste) it before.

9. _____ (you + ever + meet) my friend Dolly?

10. RICHARD: Are you taking Professor Snape's class this semester?

NICOLE: No, I _____ (already + take) it twice.

I _____ (fail) it in October,

and I _____ (take) it again last semester.

11. PIERRE: Do you do much traveling?

MARTHA: Yes, it's really one of those things that make me happy.

PIERRE: What countries _____ (you + go) to?

MARTHA: Well, when I was a child, my dad's job required that we travel a lot.

I _____ (be) to England, Turkey, Madagascar, Spain, and Portugal.

PIERRE: I _____ (never + be) to Turkey or Madagascar.

When _____ (you + be) in Madagascar?

MARTHA: Three years ago. I _____ (also + visit) the neighboring

islands. I _____ (take) a boat tour that lasted two weeks.

PIERRE: What were the names of the islands that _____
(you + visit)?

MARTHA: I can't remember anymore. The names _____ (be) quite

difficult to pronounce, so I _____ (have) a very difficult time

memorizing them.

PIERRE: I _____ (always + want) to go abroad,

but I _____ (not + have) the opportunity to do so.

I _____ (go) to Senegal three years ago, but

I _____ (not + travel) since then.

# The past perfect

The past perfect tense expresses an action that began in the past and ended in the past. It is called the **past perfect** because the auxiliary *have* is conjugated in the past tense.

> Until yesterday evening, I **had** never **seen** that movie.
> The cat simply left the house. Someone **had forgotten** to shut the back door.
> He **had** already **showered** when we arrived.

When the conjunctions *before* or *after* are used to introduce a clause, the past perfect is rarely necessary, because the time relationship is already established and is usually clear. However, the past perfect may be used, even though the simple past suffices. Compare the following sets of examples.

> Catherine **had arrived before** we called her.
> Catherine **arrived before** we called her.

> **After** Anna **had left**, I went for a walk.
> **After** Anna **left**, I went for a walk.

---

### EXERCISE
### 5·5

*Read each sentence and think about the time relationship established by the verb forms, then answer the question that follows.*

EXAMPLE    Peter was leaving the gym when I got there. Elizabeth had left the gym when I got there.

Whom did I run into when I got to the gym?  ___*Peter*___

1. Ralph was walking into the kitchen when the cell phone rang. Pedro walked into the kitchen after the cell phone rang.

   Who expected the cell phone to ring? _____

2. Mrs. Wilson taught at UT-Arlington for eight years. Mr. Prince has taught at UT-Arlington for eight years.

   Who is teaching at UT-Arlington now? _____

3. Tyler went to buy groceries because he was running out of food. Robin went to buy groceries because he had run out of food.

   Who is planning ahead? _____

4. When it stopped snowing, Lucas was walking to the bus stop. When it stopped snowing, Bertrand walked to the bus stop.

   Which of the two probably caught a cold? _____

5. Lucy was leaving the room when I walked in. Ruben had left the room when I walked in.

   Whom did I run into when entering the room? _____

6. She looked across the street, and Paul was waving at her. She looked across the street, and Fabien waved at her.

   Who had already started waving at her before she looked across the street?

   _____

7. Lucas put on a jacket because he had been waiting at the bus stop for too long. Bertrand put on a jacket because he was waiting at the bus stop.

Who was the first one to put on his jacket? _____

8. When I finally made it to the restaurant, Alicia had already ordered a cocktail. When I finally made it to the restaurant, Marie ordered a cocktail.

Who was drinking when I finally made it to the restaurant? _____

9. Kenji lived in Tokyo for two years. His uncle has been living in Okinawa for twelve years.

Who is still living in Japan? _____

EXERCISE
5·6

*Complete each sentence, using either the simple past or the past perfect tense of the verb(s) in parentheses. In some cases, either tense is possible.*

EXAMPLE    She __*had already finished*__ (already + finish) her graduate studies before
she __*turned*__ (turn) 21 years old.

1. There was a strong wind and it was raining hard, but by the time my shift at work

_____ (be) over, the storm _____ (stop).

2. The anthropologist _____ (leave) the Yucatan region

once she _____ (collect) enough information and

_____ (record) a decent amount of data.

3. I was late. Professor Griffin _____ (already + give)

a quiz when I _____ (get) to class.

She _____ (also + hand out) the syllabus for next semester.

4. I _____ (feel) much better after I _____

(take) the aspirin you _____ (give) me.

5. He _____ (be) a curator for the Metropolitan Museum before

he _____ (become) a writer.

6. Sophie _____ (lock) herself out of the apartment.

She _____ (walk out) the door thinking she

_____ (take) everything she would need for the day. In the rush,

she _____ (forget) her keys on the kitchen counter.

7. Up until then, it _____ (be) a beautiful day. But when we finally

_____ (make) it to the gates of Yosemite National Park, the clouds

_____ (block out) the sun and the scenery was no longer charming.

*Had* used as an auxiliary verb is commonly contracted with personal pronouns when people speak or write informally: *I'd, he'd,* and so on.

EXERCISE
5·7

*Complete each sentence, using either the simple past or the past perfect tense of the verb(s) in parentheses.*

1. Yesterday at a bar, I _____ (run) into Janet, an old friend of mine from college. I _____ (not + see) her in almost five years. I immediately _____ (recognize) her even though she _____ (change) her hair color and _____ (lose) at least five kilos.

2. I almost missed my train. All the other passengers _____ (already + occupy) all the cabins in my assigned car by the time I _____ (buy) my ticket and _____ (make) my way to the platform.

3. I _____ (never + see) any of Ansel Adams' photographs before I _____ (visit) the Boston Museum of Fine Arts.

4. Millions of years ago, dinosaurs _____ (roam) the planet, but they _____ (become) extinct by the time humankind _____ (evolve).

5. The meeting _____ (already + begin) by the time I _____ (get) there, so I quietly _____ (sit down) in the back row and _____ (try) to catch up with the ongoing topic of discussion.

# The future perfect

The future perfect tense expresses an action that will begin and end in the future. It is formed with the future tense of *have* plus a past participle: *he will have understood.*

> I will move to Boston in July. I will see you in September. By the time we meet again, I **will have moved** to Boston.
> She **will have finished** painting the kitchen before she goes out to have dinner with Paul.
> She **will** already **have eaten** when I get there.

*Complete each sentence by changing the verb(s) in parentheses to the appropriate tense(s).*

EXAMPLE    We're ten minutes late. By the time we get to the movie theater, the movie
____*will have already begun*____ (already + begin) and we ____*will miss*____ (miss)
the beginning of the story.

1. This traffic is terrible. We're going to miss the departure of the Greyhound bus. By the time
we _____ (get) to the Greyhound station, the bus I need to take
_____ (already + leave) the station.

2. Merrick and Toy got married last October. It's January, and Merrick and Toy
_____ (be) married for four months. By December,
they _____ (be) married for three months. By February,
they _____ (be) married for five months.

3. We have been together for a long time. By my next birthday, we
_____ (be) dating for three and a half years.

4. What? He broke his ankle again? At this rate, he _____ (suffer)
two dozen fractures by the time he _____ (retire) from triathlon
competitions.

5. I don't understand how those triathlon competitors do it. They began the race three hours
ago. By the time they get to the finish line, they _____ (run)
and _____ (swim) nonstop for eight hours!

6. Go ahead and take the day off. By tomorrow morning,
I _____ (take) care of those court cases for you.

7. The traffic was awful this afternoon. By the time we _____ (get)
to the Greyhound bus station, Mike's bus _____
(already + arrive).

8. This morning, I came to visit my grandmother at ten o'clock. It is almost 11 and I am still
walking in the park with my grandmother. I _____ (walk) with
my grandmother for an hour. By ten thirty, I _____ (walk) with
my grandmother for half an hour. By noon, I _____ (walk)
with my grandmother for two hours.

9. Jules was born in 1950. By the year 2010, he _____ (live) in Berlin
for 60 years.

10. I'm so tired of sitting on this plane. Do you realize that by the time we arrive in Tokyo,

we _____ (travel) for 20 hours straight?

*Complete each sentence, using appropriate tense(s) for the verb(s) in parentheses.*

1. Tomorrow, after he _____ (go) to the movies,

   Tyler _____ (meet) Barbara for a drink downtown.

   This means that by the time he _____ (meet) Barbara,

   he _____ (watch) the movie.

2. Since the beginning of the summer, Elizabeth _____ (read)

   three novels. Right now, she _____ (read) *1984*, a novel written

   by George Orwell. She _____ (read) it for the past two weeks.

   She _____ (intend) to finish it by next week. In her lifetime,

   she _____ (read) many science fiction novels, but this is one

   of the most fascinating novels she _____ (ever + read).

3. A couple of days ago, Elizabeth _____ (begin) to read *1984*.

   It's a dense novel. She _____ (not + finish) reading it yet. She

   _____ (read) it because one of her good friends recommended it.

4. Right now, the children _____ (take) a nap.

   They both _____ (fall) asleep an hour ago.

   They _____ (sleep) for an hour. It's likely that they

   _____ (sleep) for another half hour or so.

5. Yesterday morning, Cecilia woke up and ate breakfast. She _____

   (already + eat) breakfast when she _____ (leave) her apartment.

   She _____ (usually + try) to eat a healthy breakfast before she

   _____ (head out) to class. I usually _____

   (not + eat) breakfast before I _____ (go) to work. But I often

   _____ (get) hungry before mid-morning. Tomorrow,

   I _____ (try) something different, and before

   I _____ (go) to work, I _____ (eat)

   breakfast.

6. Cecilia is in my history class. She _____ (study) history this

   semester. She _____ (also + take) some other classes. Her classes

   _____ (begin) at eight in the morning every day.

7. Marie is in yoga class every afternoon from six to seven thirty. Three days ago,

   I _____ (go) by her apartment to see if she

   _____ (want) to jog with me around Town Lake.

8. Don't try to call Marie on her home phone at seven in the evening, because she

   _____ (attend) her yoga class at that time.

9. Yesterday, Francis _____ (lock) himself in the darkroom between

   three and four o'clock in the afternoon. I _____ (come) by

   to see him at three thirty. When I _____ (get) there, Francis

   _____ (mix) the chemicals he _____

   (use) to develop his pictures. He _____ (work) on his pictures

   for 30 minutes by the time I arrived.

EXERCISE
5·10

*Complete each sentence, using appropriate tense(s) for the verb(s) in parentheses.*

1. PAUL:  May I borrow some money? My payment _____

   (be) supposed to go through this morning, but for some reason the bank

   _____ (not + have) received it yet.

   I _____ (need) to pay my rent by six o'clock,

   but I _____ (not + have) any money.

   PATRICIA:  Sure, I'd be glad to, but I _____ (not + know) how much

   money I have in my account. How much _____ (you + need)?

   PAUL:  About 400 dollars. I promise I _____ (pay) you back as

   soon as my bank _____ (take) care of the problem.

2. PIERRE:  Hello?

   PATRICIA:  Hello, may I speak to Paul?

   PIERRE:  He _____ (not + be) at home right now, sorry.

PATRICIA: Could you please tell him that Patricia _____ (call).

If he _____ (get) home before noon, could you tell him to meet

me at Café Bourville? I _____ (sit) at one of the tables on the

terrace _____ (study) German.

3. Yesterday, while I _____ (sit) in class,

I _____ (begin) to feel ill. The person who

_____ (sit) next to me _____ (ask) me

if I was feeling okay. I _____ (try) to assure her that everything

_____ (be) okay, but she _____ (do) not

listen to me. The professor _____ (talk), and I didn't want to

interrupt him, so I just _____ (sit) there trying to focus on the

lecture. Finally, after I _____ (feel) ill for about 20 minutes,

I _____ (raise) my hand and _____ (ask)

to be excused.

4. About five hours ago, David _____ (lie) on the couch reading

a novel. Suddenly, he _____ (hear) a loud bang at the door

and _____ (get) up to see who it might be.

He _____ (look) through the peephole and then

_____ (open) the door. Someone _____

(just + leave) a book on the doormat and _____ (take off).

5. Next month, I _____ (take) a week's vacation. I haven't been able

to do so in over a year, so I _____ (really + look) forward to it.

First, I _____ (go) to the south of France to visit my brother. After

I _____ (leave) Marseille, I _____ (go) to

Berlin to see a friend who _____ (study) political science there.

Esther _____ (live) there for two years, so I presume that she

_____ (know) the city well. For whatever it's worth,

she _____ (promise) to be my tour guide while

I _____ (stay) there. I _____ (never + be)

to Europe, so I'm pretty excited about the whole trip. Berlin is one of those cities

I _____ (always + want) to visit.

*For each sentence, determine whether the form of* have *is used as a verb or as an auxiliary verb.*

EXAMPLES    They have cleaned everything.  ___auxiliary verb___

They have no money.  _____verb_____

1. He has three sisters. _____

2. She has eaten the entire cake. _____

3. They have four cats. _____

4. He had finished the exercises. _____

5. He has a pencil, but it needs sharpening. _____

6. We have run all the way over here. _____

# Modal auxiliaries

Auxiliaries can be organized into two groups. The first of these groups consists of the three high-frequency auxiliaries *be, have,* and *do.* Besides functioning as auxiliaries, they may also be used as verbs.

> Carlos **is** a marketing manager.
> Yvette **has** six children.
> The Wyatt brothers **do** business efficiently.

When *be* is used as an auxiliary verb, it is combined with a present participle.

> Carlos **is setting** goals for the year to come.

When *have* is used as an auxiliary verb, it is combined with a past participle.

> Yvette **has done** all she can to raise them.

And when *do* is used as an auxiliary, it can be used with *not* to negate a statement; it can also introduce a question or add emphasis to a statement.

> The Wyatt brothers **do**n't **like** to lose their investors.
> **Do** you **spend** a lot of time at the library?
> We **do go** to the library on Saturdays, if not during the week.

A second group of auxiliaries is the **modal auxiliaries**. Some of the most frequently used modal auxiliaries are *be to, be supposed to, may, might, must, can, could, had better, have to, have got to, ought to, should, used to,* and *would.* For the most part, these auxiliaries express the speaker's mind-set or mood. In addition, modal auxiliaries may indicate possibility, permission, obligation, or ability.

> They **should** talk to their parents about it.
> Every morning I **would** drive 15 miles to work.
> I **might** be able to finish the kitchen by tonight.

Modal auxiliaries always precede the verb in the sentence, regardless of the verb form, including the addition of the auxiliaries *be, have,* and *do.* Modal auxiliaries (except those that include *be* or *have*) do not change form for number, and some make no tense changes.

When used in the present tense, most modal auxiliaries are followed by the base form of the verb.

> Mom **might make** fried chicken tonight.
> They **must consider** every possibility.

33

In order to form a question with a modal auxiliary, move the auxiliary to the beginning of the sentence in front of the subject.

> **Can** you lift this heavy box?
> **May** our friends join you for lunch?

To form a negative statement with a modal auxiliary, place the word *not* immediately after the modal auxiliary and before all other auxiliary verbs.

> I **cannot** understand a word she says.
> Maybe she **should not** have borrowed that winter jacket.

*Would* and *could* specify a desired or hypothetical situation. These two auxiliaries are often used in a main clause when *if* + a subjunctive form is used in the other clause.

> He **would** really like to eat one.
> I wish I **could** go horse riding.
> If I were a rich man, I **would** build homeless shelters everywhere.

*Would* is also used to indicate a habitual action.

> I **would** often go to the movies with my sister.

*Can* indicates the ability to do something. Note that its past form is *could*.

> Walking down that road **can** be dangerous.
> Man **can** travel far into outer space.
> She **could** not see where the road ended.

Whereas *can* indicates the ability to do something, *may* indicates that something is acceptable. In casual speech, however, *can* is often substituted for *may*.

> Anne **may** borrow my car if she needs to.
> Anne **can** borrow my car if she needs to.

The first sentence above indicates that Anne has permission to borrow the car, while the second sentence indicates that Anne has the ability to borrow it, or, if used casually, that she has permission to borrow it.

Although there is no clear-cut rule, *may* is usually used to make polite requests.

> **May** I have one of those forms, please?
> Dad, **may** we go swimming today?

*Must* indicates necessity or requirement; it can also express certainty.

> We **must** obtain a license before we can sell liquor.
> I **must** insist that you finish the job by dusk.
> If he's not here, he **must** have been delayed.

*May* and *might* can both indicate uncertainty or possibility.

> I **may** have to go to New York this weekend.
> The children **may** need a flu shot.
> We **might** have another storm tonight.
> You **might** be right.

*Had better* and *ought to* suggest that something needs to be done and imply advisability.

> You **had better** be on time for your own party.
> She really **ought to** find new friends.

EXERCISE
6·1

*Underline the correct modal auxiliary in each sentence.*

1. It's raining, and you **may** | **might** not play outside.

2. His father **should** | **may** not believe him blindly.

3. Don't send the e-mail out, because I **might** | **must** change my mind.

4. **Would** | **Should** we leave the clothes to dry outside?

5. If they rehearsed more often, they **may** | **would** become a good rock band.

6. He **can** | **may** play basketball really well, and he's a good student as well.

7. No one **can** | **must** play the drums better than John.

8. The hurricane **should** | **could** cause a lot of damage if it hits the coast.

9. They **may** | **must** go hiking tomorrow if the weather is nice.

10. You **could** | **should** not play with knives or guns.

EXERCISE
6·2

*Complete each sentence with an appropriate phrase.*

EXAMPLE     You must ____*learn to respect your elders*____.

1. He can _____.

2. She would _____.

3. I should _____.

4. You ought to _____.

5. He had better _____.

6. May I _____?

7. Can you please _____?

8. Why must that man _____?

*Complete each sentence with either* must *or* should.

EXAMPLE   They ___*should*___ buy organic fruit, because it's healthier.

1. We _____ go to India for our spring vacation.

2. If you want to become a lawyer, you _____ go to law school.

3. A child _____ drink at least three glasses of milk a day.

4. A person _____ eat a balanced diet.

5. A person _____ eat in order to live.

6. According to my academic advisor, I _____ take another history course.

7. I _____ pay my bills online tonight, but I think I'll wait and do it in the morning.

8. Everyone _____ have a goal in life.

9. You _____ have a passport issued before you can leave the country.

10. Wheat _____ have plenty of sun in order to grow.

11. If the car is locked, you _____ use a key to open it.

12. I _____ go to work, but I don't feel well. I think I'll stay home.

13. I just missed the last bus, so I _____ walk home.

14. If you don't know how to pronounce a word, you _____ ask a native speaker of English to pronounce it for you.

15. This cake is very good. You _____ try a piece.

16. This cake is excellent! You _____ try a piece!

# Shades of meaning

*Ought to* and *had better* express advisability. But besides expressing advisability, *ought to,* as well as *should,* may suggest that care be taken in carrying out the action of the verb. In addition, they may imply duty or responsibility in carrying out that action.

| | |
|---|---|
| ADVISABILITY | You **ought to** stay here till the storm ends. |
| | You **had better** stay here till the storm ends. |
| SUGGESTION | You **should** try harder. |
| | You **ought to** try harder. |
| DUTY OR RESPONSIBILITY | Children **should** follow the school's safety regulations. |
| | Children **ought to** follow the school's safety regulations. |

*Had better* is similar in meaning to *ought to* and *should,* but it is usually stronger. The auxiliary *had better* often expresses a warning. It is followed by the basic form of the verb and has either a present or future meaning.

Our left front tire is almost flat. We **had better** stop to fill it with air.
She **had better** clean that wound as soon as possible, or it might get infected.

Like the auxiliary verb *had*, the verb *had* in the auxiliary *had better* can contract with a subject pronoun: *you'd better, they'd better,* and so on.

The past form of *should* is composed of *should have* + past participle.

I had an exam this morning. I didn't do well on it, because I read the wrong chapter.
I **should have been** more attentive in class.
It feels like I really hurt my ankle. I **should not have played** soccer for so long this afternoon.

The past form of *ought to* is composed of *ought to have* + past participle.

I **ought to have read** the right chapter.
You **ought to have thought** about the consequences before you volunteered.

### EXERCISE
### 6·4

*For each pair of sentences, select the one that is stronger in meaning or shows greater obligation.*

1. a. You'd better not go out there alone.
   b. You shouldn't go out there alone.

2. a. She shouldn't go into that room.
   b. She must not go into that room.

3. a. I should call the police.
   b. I have to call the police.

4. a. They must go to class.
   b. They ought to go to class.

5. a. You should go to the doctor.
   b. You had better go to the doctor.

6. a. He has to go to work.
   b. He ought to go to work.

### EXERCISE
### 6·5

*Respond to each sentence, using the past form* should have *or* should not have.

EXAMPLE    You forgot to set your alarm clock, because you fell asleep on the couch.
    *I shouldn't have fallen asleep on the couch.*

1. You didn't do your exercises, because you went to a movie.

   _____

2. You failed the exam, because you didn't study.

   _____

3. You didn't read the chapter, because you played video games instead.

_____

4. You misspelled a word, because you didn't look it up in the dictionary.

_____

5. The room is full of mosquitoes, because you left the window open.

_____

6. It's warm in here, because you turned off the fan.

_____

7. You're poor, because you spent all your money while you were on vacation.

_____

8. You can't make dinner, because you didn't go grocery shopping.

_____

9. You are cold, because you left your coat at home.

_____

10. You can't look her in the eye, because you lied to her.

_____

11. You didn't have coffee this morning. You're feeling very sleepy.

_____

12. You have a stomachache, because you ate all the ice cream.

_____

*Have to* and *have got to* express necessity. Like *must,* they suggest that there is no other choice.

> All candidates **have to** take the grammar test.
> I simply **have got to** get there on time.

In informal conversation, *must* usually carries a stronger connotation than *have to* and often indicates a sense of urgency.

> I **have to** speak to Robert. I was hoping we could get together for lunch.
> I **must** speak to Robert immediately. His brother was in a car accident.

The past tense of *have to* is *had to.*

> I **have to** leave by tomorrow morning.
> I **had to** leave by this morning.

*Have to* and *must,* when in the negative, express lack of necessity or prohibition. *Do not have to* indicates that something is unnecessary, while *must not* indicates that something is not allowed.

> Tomorrow is Christmas, and we **do not have to** go to work.
> You **must not** tamper with that device.

EXERCISE
**6·6**

*Complete each sentence with either* must not (mustn't) *or* do/does not have to (don't/doesn't have to).

EXAMPLE    He's already finished painting the kitchen, so I ___*do not have to*___ paint anymore.

1. I've already finished all my reading for tomorrow, so I _____ study tonight. I will go to the movies instead.

2. I _____ forget to take my key with me before leaving. I could get locked out of my apartment.

3. The second part of the exam is optional. She _____ take it, but she probably should.

4. Polar bears are beautiful animals. We _____ allow them to become extinct.

5. If you get bitten by a snake, you _____ panic, because it will accelerate your pulse and your blood circulation. This will cause the venom to travel faster through your body.

6. This is a one-time opportunity to get the job you've always dreamed of. You _____ let it pass you by. Accept the offer.

7. Dolphins _____ see in order to avoid obstacles like fishing boats. Even in complete darkness, they would be able to navigate around them.

8. When crossing borders in Europe, one _____ declare merchandise anymore. The new border regulations set by the European Union are looser.

9. We _____ go see that play if you don't want to, but from what I understand, it's really good.

10. You _____ play with matches. Look around you, Peter, this house is entirely made out of wood.

11. A person _____ own a three-story house or a minivan to be happy.

12. She really doesn't feel well. We _____ wait until she has a fever to call the doctor. We _____ wait any longer to take her to the hospital.

13. In order to make friends, you _____ be rude.

14. You _____ be a genius to learn English.

15. You _____ lend me their new album. I was able to buy it in advance four weeks ago, so I've already heard it several times.

*Be supposed to* and *be to* express expectation. They suggest that someone is expecting something about a scheduled situation, the fulfillment of conditions, or the use of proper procedures.

If used in conversation, *be to* is usually stronger in meaning and more clear-cut than *be supposed to*.

> The plane **is supposed to** take off in an hour.
> The plane **is to** take off at ten in the morning.

In the first example, the speaker expects the flight to take off in an hour, because that's when it is scheduled to depart. The second sentence is similar in meaning to the first sentence, but it states a fact. The speaker knows with certainty when the plane will be taking off.

*Be to* and *be supposed to* can also express expectation about behavior.

> I **am supposed to** go to this meeting. My director told me he would be pleased to see me there.
> I **am to be** at this meeting. My director told us it is mandatory.

EXERCISE
6·7

*Rewrite each sentence, beginning with* You are (not) to.

EXAMPLE    Do not enter private property.

_You are not to enter private property._

1. Keep off the grass. _____

2. No eating or drinking inside. _____

3. Move to the rear of the plane. _____

4. Do not feed the monkeys. _____

5. No smoking. _____

6. No visitors allowed on board. _____

7. No littering. _____

8. Do not use the elevator in case of fire. _____

*Used to* expresses a habitual action in the past, one that is no longer performed or repeated. *Used to* can be used interchangeably with *would* in this sense. However, since *would* also has other meanings, it requires an indication of past time to make sense. Compare the following sets of examples.

> I **used to** go surfing every summer.
> When I was a teenager, I **would** go surfing every summer.

> I **used to** run five miles every morning.
> Before I broke my knee, I **would** run five miles every morning.

# Special auxiliaries

In modern English, *shall* has generally been replaced by *will*. In the past, *shall* was used as the first-person form of *will* to express the future tense. Nowadays, *shall* is usually used in a context where the speaker wishes to sound very polite or very formal.

When *shall* and *will* are used in questions, however, their meanings differ greatly. *Will* indicates the future tense, while *shall* (when used before *I* or *we*) means that the speaker is making a suggestion or asking someone else whether he or she agrees with the suggestion being made.

> **Will** we drive to the nearest gas station?
> **Will** we get a cup of tea?
>
> **Shall** we drive to the nearest gas station?
> Let's go, **shall** we?

*Let's* (*let us*) and *why don't* are modal auxiliaries that are used to make suggestions or friendly or polite commands.

> **Let's** go to a movie.
> **Why don't** you pick me up at eight or so?

**EXERCISE 6·8**

*In each sentence, underline the modal auxiliary that more appropriately introduces the question.*

EXAMPLE    **Can** | **May** I take you to the movies?

1. **Can** | **May** you explain this magic trick to me?

2. **Can** | **May** I offer you coffee?

3. **Will** | **Shall** we have to pay a cover charge to get into this club?

4. **Will** | **Shall** we go the beach if it's still sunny?

5. **Can** | **May** you give me directions to Paul's house?

6. **Will** | **Shall** they let us use the swimming pool?

7. Let's dance, **can** | **shall** we?

**EXERCISE 6·9**

*For each pair of sentences, select the one that is stronger in meaning.*

1. a. We had better bring some water.
   b. We should bring some water.

2. a. We ought to bring some water.
   b. We have got to bring some water.

3. a. You have got to drink water.
   b. You should drink water.

4. a. You are to drink water.
   b. You ought to drink water.

5. a. You must drink water.
   b. You had better drink water.

6. a. You were supposed to bring some water.
   b. You had to bring some water.

7. a. You are supposed to bring some water.
   b. You are to bring some water.

# The progressive forms of modal auxiliaries

The present progressive form of a modal auxiliary is composed of a modal auxiliary + *be* + verb form ending in *-ing*. The meaning consists of the meaning of the modal auxiliary and that of the present-tense progressive form of the verb.

In the example below, the speaker wonders (*may*) whether Sophie is resting.

> We should probably come back later. Sophie **may be resting**.

In the example below, the speaker believes (*must*) that the store is closing.

> The lights inside are being turned off. The store **must be closing**.

The past progressive form is composed of a modal auxiliary + *have been* + verb form ending in *-ing*. The meaning consists of the meaning of the modal auxiliary and that of the past-tense progressive form of the verb.

In the example below, the speaker suspects (*might*) that Diana was sleeping in.

> Diana wasn't at church today. She **might have been sleeping** in.

In the example below, the speaker believes (*must*) that Paul was studying all night.

> Paul looked tired this morning. He **must have been studying** all night.

By using a modal auxiliary, a speaker is choosing to express a degree of certainty or uncertainty. The degree of certainty reflects how sure the speaker is of something happening or how true his or her statement might be. If the speaker is sure of something, he or she doesn't use a modal.

> He is sick.

If the speaker wants to express a strong degree of certainty, he or she uses *must*.

> He **must be** sick.

If the speaker wants to express a weak degree of certainty, he or she uses *may, might,* or *could*:

> He **may be** sick.

Complete each sentence, using the verb in parentheses with the modal auxiliary that best expresses the degree of certainty of the statement (must, should, may, could, or might). Use the correct progressive form of the verb.

EXAMPLE    Serge seems very busy these days. He ___may be finishing___ (finish) his doctoral dissertation.

1. Don't be mad at Henry. He didn't mean to offend you. I think he

   _____ (kid).

2. Sorry for the noise. Olivia is upstairs with her friends, and they

   _____ (play) some sort of game that requires running

   around a lot.

3. I am wasting time right now. I am playing video games, but I

   _____ (study). I have a final in Economics first thing

   in the morning.

4. I really need to speak to Peter right away, but I can't remember what hotel he told me he

   would be staying in. He _____ (stay) at the Hilton, but I'm not

   sure. He _____ (stay) at the Concorde.

5. Don't be mad at Henry. Although I am not sure, I doubt he meant to offend you.

   He _____ (kid) when he said that, but who knows?

6. All the people coming into the restaurant are carrying wet umbrellas.

   It _____ (rain) outside.

7. I am not sure whether Marie is in her room or not. She _____
   (jog) around the park like she usually does at this time of the day.

8. I smell smoke. Something _____ (burn).

9. He is over an hour late, but I don't know for sure where he could be.

   He _____ (ride) the bus over here, which will take him

   a while. Or he _____ (walk), in which case I doubt he will

   be here in time for dinner.

10. I heard he hurt himself while rock climbing. He _____ (climb)
    without supervision.

The distinction between two forms of modal auxiliaries needs to be clarified: *used to* and *be used to*. *Used to* expresses a "habitual past," an activity or a situation that existed in the past but no longer exists. It is formed by using *used to* + base form of the verb.

Alfred **used to work** for IBM.
My family **used to vacation** in Maryland.

*Be used to* is equivalent in meaning to "be familiar with" or "be accustomed to." Both *be used to* and *be accustomed to* can be followed by a **gerund** (a verb form ending in -*ing*), a noun phrase, or a pronoun.

> Kevin grew up in Alaska, so he **is used to living** in cold weather.
> I think I**'m** finally **used to working** nights.
> He **wasn't used to** such rude behavior.
> I**'m** finally **used to** it.

The modal auxiliaries *would* and *used to* are interchangeable when they express a habitual past.

> My brother and I **used to** go skiing every morning.
> My brother and I **would** go skiing every morning.

However, when *used to* expresses a situation or state of being in the past, it cannot be replaced by *would*. This occurs most frequently with the verb *be*. The modal auxiliary *would* can only be used to express a recurring action in the past.

> I **used to be** a firefighter.  (**Would** *cannot be used.*)
> **Did**n't you **used to be** a flight attendant?  (**Would** *cannot be used.*)

**EXERCISE**

**7·2**

*For each sentence, determine if a form of the verb* be *is required. If so, write the correct form in the blank. If not, mark an X in the blank.*

EXAMPLE   Chris rides his bike everywhere. He ___*is*___ used to biking long distances.

1. A teacher _____ used to correcting exercises quickly. Students often turn them in at the last minute.

2. People _____ used to think the earth was the center of the universe.

3. Peter _____ used to do all the house chores, because he lived alone. Now he has a roommate, so he only has to clean the dishes and sweep the floor.

4. In the American West, horses _____ used to be the main means of transportation.

   Today, hardly anyone uses horses. Instead, they travel by plane, because they _____

   used to faster forms of transportation.

5. I have lived in South Africa for a long time. I _____ used to high temperatures.

6. I _____ used to live in the south of England, but now I live in Spain.

7. They _____ used to sitting outside when they eat. During the summer, they always sit at that picnic table.

8. When I was a teenager, I _____ used to smoke cigarettes. I quit a long time ago, though.

9. It's too bad they closed the corner store. Alex and I _____ used to stopping by there to buy bottled water on our way to the basketball court.

10. I _____ used to sitting in the back of the bus, but I don't mind sitting in the front.

11. Chris has never owned a car. He _____ used to taking public transportation.

12. Maria and I are from different cultures. She _____ used to having eggs for breakfast.

   I _____ used to drinking coffee and running out the door.

*Complete each sentence, using the appropriate form of* would *or* used to *with the verb in parentheses.*

EXAMPLE    I ___*used to be*___ (be) able to read two or three books a week.

1. I _____ (be) scared of sleeping with my door closed. Whenever I got

   ready for bed, I _____ (open) it.

2. Famine is still a problem in most of East Africa, but it _____ (be) more
   widespread than it is now.

3. I got a huge red kite when I was 12. My friend Chris _____ (ask) to

   borrow it so he could fly it too, but for months I _____ (never + let)

   any of my friends use it.

4. I remember my third-grade math teacher really well. Every morning, he

   _____ (begin) class by telling us how important mathematics

   was in everyday life.

5. I _____ (be) a political science major. After graduating, I was hired

   to work at the United Nations. Every Wednesday morning, our council

   _____ (get together) and discuss articles from the local newspaper.

   After that, we _____ (go) to the cafeteria and have breakfast together.

   Back then, I _____ (drink) at least two cups of coffee a day, but now

   I only drink tea.

6. I _____ (be) very selfish. Whenever someone asked me for a favor,

   I _____ (make up) an excuse and I _____

   (not + help) them.

7. I _____ (be) scared of heights. My heart _____

   (start) racing and I _____ (have) trouble catching my breath. Now I am

   used to it.

8. When I was in middle school, I _____ (take) my soccer ball with me
   every morning to play with the other kids.

9. When my grandmother was a girl, her mother _____ (walk) her to school every day.

10. Last summer my friend Mike and I went to Big Bend National Park. We had the greatest of times. Every afternoon, we _____ (swim) in the river,

we _____ (dry out) while sitting in the sun, and then we

_____ (get ready) for dinner. If we weren't too tired, we

_____ (hike) back to the camp instead of using our motorbikes.

11. I can remember Mrs. Limon well. She was my neighbor when I _____

(live) in San Francisco. She _____ (always + smile) and

_____ (say) hello to me whenever I'd run into her on my way home.

When I talked to her for too long, she _____ (clear) her throat.

That was her way of telling me that she needed to get back to what she was doing.

# The auxiliary verb *do*

As an auxiliary verb, *do* (*does/did*) is typically used to form questions and negative statements. Sometimes *do* is used to emphasize contradiction to something that has already been said.

> For the most part I don't like dogs, but I **do** like my father's German shepherd.

## Using *do* in questions

There are two types of questions: **closed questions** (also called **yes/no questions**) and **information questions**. Yes/no questions, as the name suggests, are questions that can be answered by *yes* or *no*.

> **Does** he live in New York? **Yes**, he **does**.
> **Do** they understand English? **No**, they **don't**.
> **Did** you get my letter? **No**, I **didn't**.

Information questions are open questions that ask for information by using a question word.

> **Where does** he live? He lives in New York.
> **When did** she arrive? She arrived yesterday.

A specific pattern is generally employed to form information questions: question word + *do* + subject + main verb. *Does* is used in questions where the subject is in the third-person singular (*he, she, it*). *Do* is used with all other persons. *Did* is used in the past tense.

> Where **does** she live? She lives here.
> Where **do** they live? They live here.
> Where **did** he live? He lived here.

EXERCISE
8·1

*For each sentence, write a closed question, then write an information question using* where.

EXAMPLE    She exercises in this gym.

   *Does she exercise in this gym?*

   *Where does she exercise?*

1. They come here.

   _____

   _____

2. She stayed here.

   _____

   _____

3. His airplane landed in the morning.

   _____

   _____

4. The package arrived.

   _____

   _____

5. Robert lives there.

   _____

   _____

# Using *do* in negative sentences

There are affirmative sentences (*The moon is white.*), and there are negative sentences (*The moon is* not *white.*). The word *not* is used to express negation. Except for the verb *be* and auxiliaries, verbs require a form of the auxiliary *do* to make a negative statement.

> He **is not** at home at the moment.
> You **must not** play ball in the street.

BUT

> They **do not speak** a word of Spanish.
> The students **did not have** enough time for the exam.

Negative verb phrases are generally formed as follows.

| AUXILIARY + *not* + VERB PHRASE | | | SENTENCE |
|---|---|---|---|
| do | not | go there | I **do not go** there. |
| does | not | go there | He **does not go** there. |
| did | not | go there | James **did not go** there. |

It is common to combine *do, does,* and *did* with *not* to form a contraction.

> I **don't** go there.
> He **doesn't** go there.
> James **didn't** go there.

There are other negative adverbs in addition to *not: rarely, never, seldom, scarcely (ever),* *hardly (ever),* and *barely (ever).*

You should avoid using **double negatives**. Whereas writing "I *do not* have any money" is grammatically correct, writing (or even saying) "I *do not* have *no* money" is confusing and grammatically incorrect, because it contains two negatives in the same clause (*do not* + *no*). A clause should contain only one negative (*do not* or *no*).

EXERCISE
8·2

*Make each sentence negative by using* not . . . any.

EXAMPLE      They have many financial debts.

_They do not have any financial debts._

1. I own black-and-white movies.

_____

2. I have problems with my computer.

_____

3. We have time to waste.

_____

4. I saw a person I know.

_____

5. I need help with my homework.

_____

6. I trust some of you.

_____

7. I trust someone.

_____

EXERCISE
8·3

*For each sentence, write a yes/no question, then change it to a negative question. Retain the tense of the original sentence.*

EXAMPLE      Tom works in New York.

_Does Tom work in New York?_

_Doesn't Tom work in New York?_

1. The girls need some help.

_____

_____

2. She has a job in a bakery.

_____

_____

3. Bob saw somebody in the shadows.

_____

_____

4. I like hot tea.

_____

_____

*For each sentence, determine whether the form of* do *is used as a verb or as an auxiliary verb.*

EXAMPLES     I do not like eating strawberries. _____auxiliary verb_____

Marie did her homework over. _____verb_____

1. They are doing their exercises. _____

2. He does not like the countryside. _____

3. She does nothing all day. _____

4. Did you finish your dinner? _____

5. I am doing what I was asked to do. _____

6. Did she make it on time? _____

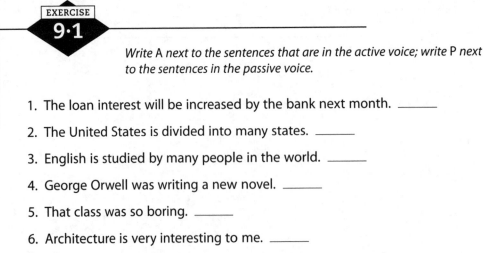

# The passive voice

·9·

In English, most sentences can be written in two ways: in the **active voice** or in the **passive voice**. Active-voice sentences can contain a subject, a transitive verb, and an object.

> Paul **wrote** the essay.
> My sister **reads** my diary.

In a passive-voice sentence, the subject and object of an active-voice sentence switch positions; the active object becomes the subject of the passive sentence, and the active subject becomes the object of the preposition *by*. The verb from the active sentence is changed to a past participle and is used with the auxiliary *be*.

> The essay **was written** by Paul.
> My diary **is read** by my sister.

The meaning of these active and passive examples is essentially the same. They are simply two different ways of expressing the same action. Although the active voice is the way you learn to write correct complete sentences, the passive voice is common in written English, especially in formal academic writing, and in newspapers and magazines.

EXERCISE
**9·1**

*Write A next to the sentences that are in the active voice; write P next to the sentences in the passive voice.*

1. The loan interest will be increased by the bank next month. _____

2. The United States is divided into many states. _____

3. English is studied by many people in the world. _____

4. George Orwell was writing a new novel. _____

5. That class was so boring. _____

6. Architecture is very interesting to me. _____

7. I was so surprised by his sudden decision to leave. _____

8. He was pushed by the man in the trench coat. _____

9. The tsunami happened in Southeast Asia. _____

# Using the passive

The passive voice occurs in all tenses and can even be used in a progressive tense. The following examples show active sentences and their corresponding passive formations.

|  | ACTIVE | PASSIVE |
|---|---|---|
| SIMPLE PRESENT | Eric **carries** Pam. | Pam **is carried** by Eric. |
| PRESENT PROGRESSIVE | Eric **is carrying** Pam. | Pam **is being carried** by Eric. |
| SIMPLE PAST | Eric **carried** Pam. | Pam **was carried** by Eric. |
| PAST PROGRESSIVE | Eric **was carrying** Pam. | Pam **was being carried** by Eric. |
| PRESENT PERFECT | Eric **has carried** Pam. | Pam **has been carried** by Eric. |
| PAST PERFECT | Eric **had carried** Pam. | Pam **had been carried** by Eric. |
| SIMPLE FUTURE | Eric **will carry** Pam. | Pam **will be carried** by Eric. |
| FUTURE PERFECT | Eric **will have carried** Pam. | Pam **will have been carried** by Eric. |
| "be going to" FORM | Eric **is going to carry** Pam. | Pam **is going to be carried** by Eric. |

When a sentence is changed from active to passive, the tense of the active sentence is retained in the passive sentence.

Patrick **paints** a picture.     A picture **is painted** by Patrick.
Samantha **is teaching** the class.     The class **is being taught** by Samantha.
Robin **borrowed** a dollar.     A dollar **was borrowed** by Robin.
Tyler **has seen** this episode.     This episode **has been seen** by Tyler.
Alicia **will prepare** a salad.     A salad **will be prepared** by Alicia.

EXERCISE
9·2

*Rewrite each active sentence as a passive sentence, retaining the tense of the original sentence.*

1. Maria found a hundred dollars.

   _____

2. The students will memorize the Preamble to the Constitution.

   _____

3. Did you purchase the tickets?

   _____

4. They have discovered some ancient ruins.

   _____

5. Bill is measuring the room.

   _____

# Sentences that cannot be written in the passive voice

Only transitive verbs—verbs followed by an object—can be used in the passive. It is not possible to use intransitive verbs, such as *happen, sleep, come, go, live, occur, rain, rise, depart, walk,* and *seem,* in the passive.

| ACTIVE VOICE | PASSIVE VOICE |
| --- | --- |
| Marie helped Peter. | Peter was helped by Marie. (TRANSITIVE VERB) |
| The baby slept soundly. | — (INTRANSITIVE VERB) |
| The student came to class. | — (INTRANSITIVE VERB) |

# Forming the passive voice without a *by* phrase

The passive is often used when it is unimportant to know who or what performs the action. In the sentence "Coffee *is grown* in Colombia," we are informed where coffee is grown. Yet the coffee could be grown by villagers, by children, by immigrants, or by any other group of people. Following are examples that illustrate the most common ways of using the passive voice without a prepositional phrase introduced with *by*.

Rice **is grown** throughout Asia.
That car **was built** in the 1930s.
This watch **was imported** from Geneva, Switzerland.
Poor Mr. Lowry **is going to be fired**!

When the subject of an active sentence is some vague entity (*they, someone, people*), it is common to avoid using a *by* phrase in the passive.

ACTIVE   **They** cultivate grapes in southern France.
PASSIVE   Grapes are cultivated in southern France.

*By* is used in the passive when it is important to inform the reader or listener who is responsible for the action: "*Perfume* was written by Patrick Süskind." In this case, it is important to know that a specific author (and not just any author) wrote this particular book.

As a general rule, if the writer knows who performs the action, it's preferable to use the active voice: "My neighbor made the strawberry pie." Stylistically, the writer could use the passive, but it would mean that he or she is trying to direct the reader's attention to the new subject: "The strawberry pie was made by my neighbor."

EXERCISE
9·3

*Rewrite each active sentence as a passive sentence. Don't use a prepositional phrase with* by.

1. They manufactured a thousand cars at that plant.

   _____

2. Many people are developing theories about that.

   _____

3. Someone will buy that painting today.

   _____

4. They have postponed the opening of the new store.

_____

5. No one respects his work.

_____

*Rewrite each active sentence as a passive sentence.*

EXAMPLE    Two horses were pulling the princess's carriage.
           *The princess's carriage was being pulled by two horses.*

1. Kevin has suggested a new design for the logo.

_____

2. The professor is going to explain the formula.

_____

3. Bartenders serve people at the bar.

_____

4. Noam Chomsky is preparing a speech.

_____

5. Alex will invite Marie to the party.

_____

6. Neil Gaiman wrote the novel *American Gods*.

_____

*Complete the second sentence of each pair with the correct passive form of the verb phrase in the first sentence. Retain the tense of the original sentence.*

EXAMPLE    William was driving the car.

           The car ___*was being*___ driven by William.

1. William will have driven the car.

   The car _____ driven by William.

2. William drives the car.

   The car _____ driven by William.

3. William is driving the car.

The car _____ driven by William.

4. William has driven the car.

The car _____ driven by William.

5. William is going to drive the car.

The car _____ driven by William.

6. William will drive the car.

The car _____ driven by William.

7. William had driven the car.

The car _____ driven by William.

EXERCISE
9·6

*Rewrite each passive sentence as an active sentence. If an active sentence is not possible, mark an X in the blank.*

EXAMPLE    The karate tournament is being sponsored by Pepsi.

*Pepsi is sponsoring the karate tournament.*

1. Technical skills are taught by every professional school in New York.

_____

2. The ping-pong tournament is being broadcast by TF1.

_____

3. The Inner Movement Symphony is being televised all over New Zealand.

_____

4. This poem was written by Keats. The other one was written by García Lorca.

_____

5. Paper was invented in China. Later, paper was produced in Baghdad by Arabs.

_____

6. The new bridge will be completed sometime next year.

_____

7. My socks were made in Scotland.

_____

*Rewrite each active sentence as a passive sentence, retaining the tense of the original sentence. Use a* by *phrase wherever possible. If a passive sentence is not possible, mark an X in the blank.*

EXAMPLE   Somebody took my chair.

_My chair was taken by somebody._

1. Someone stole my purse.

   _____

2. Garret came to New York three days ago.

   _____

3. Gabriel borrowed my fork at lunch.

   _____

4. Someone made this antique sewing machine in 1834.

   _____

5. An accident happened on Loop 1 yesterday morning.

   _____

6. Steve was watering the plants when I walked into the garden this morning.

   _____

7. The jury is going to judge the president on the basis of his testimony.

   _____

8. When did America invent the atomic bomb?

   _____

9. Caroline slept until two o'clock!

   _____

10. Is Maureen organizing a reunion this week?

    _____

11. Professionals have translated the Bible into many languages.

    _____

# The passive form of modal auxiliaries

The passive voice of modal auxiliaries is formed by the modal + *be* + past participle. This formation can be used to express the present and future tenses.

> The door **can't be opened**.
> Children **should be taught** how to read poetry.
> This package **ought to be sent** by tomorrow.
> Fred **has to be told** about the meeting.
> Jason **was supposed to be informed** about the changes.

## The future tense

With some modals, the future tense is expressed with the auxiliary *will*.

> Fred **will have to be told** about the meeting.

## The past tense

The past tense of certain modal auxiliaries in the passive voice is formed by the modal + *have been* + past participle.

> The letter **should have been sent** yesterday!
> This car **must have been stolen** two months ago.
> Andrew **ought to have been told** about the meeting.

With other modal auxiliaries, the past tense of the modal is used together with *to be* + past participle.

> Fred **had to be told** about the meeting.
> The door **couldn't be opened**.

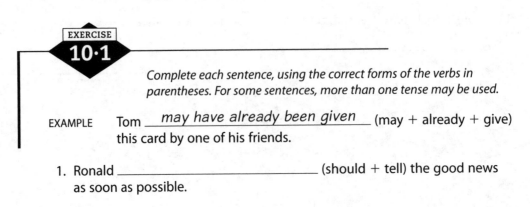

EXERCISE
**10·1**

*Complete each sentence, using the correct forms of the verbs in parentheses. For some sentences, more than one tense may be used.*

EXAMPLE    Tom _may have already been given_ (may + already + give) this card by one of his friends.

1. Ronald _____ (should + tell) the good news as soon as possible.

2. Angela _____ (should + drive) to the airport half an hour ago.

3. Someone _____ (should + clean) the kitchen before dinner.

4. Butter _____ (must + keep) in the refrigerator or it will go bad.

5. We tried talking to him, but he _____ (could + not + convince). He had already made up his mind.

6. We tried, but we _____ (could + not + open) the window.

7. I am so excited! IBM called me, and I _____ (may + offer) a job with them soon.

8. The computer firm that Stephanie interviewed with last week

   _____ (may + not + offer) her a job, even though

   she had a good feeling about it.

9. I hope Bob accepts our job offer. He _____ (may + already + offer) a job with another company.

10. It might be too late to call her with an offer. Another competing company

    _____ (may + already + hire) her.

11. Peter didn't expect to see his little brother at the party. He

    _____ (must + surprise) when he saw him drinking.

12. Today is the 8th, and his birthday was on the 2nd. Her birthday card

    _____ (should + send) a week ago.

13. His birthday is coming up next week. His present _____ (should + send) to his house soon.

14. Tricia _____ (had better + clean) her room before Mom gets back home.

15. Tricia, your room _____ (had better + clean) by the time I get home.

16. Tyler _____ (have to + return) these videos by tomorrow night.

17. These videos _____ (have to + return) to the video store by this afternoon.

18. There are too many people in this class. It _____ (ought to + divide) in two, but there are no more available classrooms.

19. Last semester's class was too large. It _____ (ought to + divide) in half.

*Complete each sentence with the correct form of the verb in parentheses together with an appropriate modal auxiliary or similar expression.*

1. He is crying. He _____ (be) sad.

2. The entire forest _____ (see) from their balcony.

3. According to our teacher, all our calculators _____ (put) into our bags before she passes out the test.

4. A child _____ (not + get) everything he asks for.

5. Your son draws quite poorly. His interest in painting _____ (not + encourage).

6. Five of the players on the team missed their plane. In my opinion, the game _____ (postpone).

7. Try to speak slowly when you give your lecture. Otherwise, some of your sentences _____ (misunderstand).

8. Some sightings of Elvis _____ (not + explain).

9. She is wearing a ring on the fourth finger of her left hand. She _____ (marry).

10. I found a wallet on the table. It _____ (left) by one of the students who was having lunch.

11. What! You lost your final paper draft? Your professor _____ (displease) once you've told him about it.

12. He is very lazy. If you need him to do something, he _____ (push).

13. The classrooms in this school are old, but the municipality gave us money and a new school _____ (build) by next summer.

14. Blue whales _____ (save) from extinction.

15. We can no longer sit here with our arms crossed! Something _____ (do)!

16. In my opinion, he _____ (elect), because he is honest and organized.

# The stative passive

Past participles in a passive-voice sentence can act like adjectives, in the sense that they describe a noun.

> The car is **old**.
> The car is **locked**.

In the first example, the word *old* is an adjective and describes *car*. In the second example, *locked* is a past participle; it functions as an adjective and also describes *car*.

Essentially, the participle is derived from passive-voice sentences like the following.

> The car **has been locked** by someone.  (The car is **locked**.)
> The window **was repaired** by someone.  (The window is **repaired**.)

## Adjectives and participles

The passive past participle can be used to describe an existing state or situation; when it does, it is called the **stative passive**. Consider the following examples.

> I locked the car door five minutes ago. Now the car door **is locked**.
> Peter broke the window two days ago. Now the window **is broken**.
> We were without water for a week. Now the pipe **is** finally **fixed**.

In all three examples, the action took place earlier, as described in the first sentence, and the state of that action in the present is expressed in the second sentence of each pair. In these second sentences, the past participle functions as an adjective.

Notice that there is no *by* phrase in any of the sentences. However, the stative passive is often followed by prepositions other than *by*.

> She is satisfied **with** her job.
> Marc is married **to** Vanessa.

There are many other common adjectives in English that are, in reality, stative passive structures.

> Frank is **interested**. I'm **bored**.
> The store was **closed**. He saw nothing but **closed** stores.
> The work was **finished**. He took the **finished** work home.

61

Following is a list of commonly used adjectives that are derived from present and past participles.

> amazing/amazed
> boring/bored
> confusing/confused
> disappointing/disappointed
> exciting/excited
> exhausting/exhausted
> frightening/frightened
> interesting/interested
> satisfying/satisfied
> surprising/surprised
> terrifying/terrified
> tiring/tired

The present participle is used as a modifier for the active voice. The past participle is used as a modifier for the passive voice.

> The athlete was **amazing**. (*This adjective describes what the athlete is.*)
> The athlete was **amazed**. (*This adjective describes what happened to the athlete.*)

> This book is **boring**. (*This adjective describes what the book is.*)
> This student is **bored**. (*This adjective describes what happened to the student.*)

EXERCISE
**11·1**

*Underline the correct participle in each sentence.*

1. The journalist was **disappointing** | **disappointed** that the newspaper didn't accept her article.

2. Tokyo is an **exciting** | **excited** international city.

3. I am very **interesting** | **interested** in astrology.

4. Reading good novels is **gratifying** | **gratified**.

5. I am sorry for messing up the sauce. The recipe was really **confusing** | **confused**.

6. Peter was also **confusing** | **confused** when he read the instructions.

7. Susan is **exciting** | **excited**, because she will see her parents soon.

8. Richard hoped that his family would be **exciting** | **excited** to meet his new girlfriend.

EXERCISE
**11·2**

*Complete each sentence, using the simple present or simple past tense of* be *with the stative passive form of the verb in parentheses.*

EXAMPLE    It's getting warm in here, because the heater ___is fixed___ (fix) again.

1. It smells bad in this kitchen, because the ventilator _____ (break).

2. It is hot in this car, because the window _____ (close).

3. Yesterday it was hot in this room, because the window _____ (close).

4. Peter is wearing a winter hat. It _____ (make) of cotton.

5. The door to the castle _____ (shut).

6. Bob looks worried. He is sitting all by himself. His elbows _____ (bend)

   and his hands _____ (fold) in front of him.

7. We can leave now, since the movie _____ (finish).

8. The headlights on his car _____ (turn) on.

9. This theater _____ (not + crowd).

10. Don't look under the stairs! Your Christmas present _____ (hide) there.

11. Oh no! How did this happen? My dress _____ (tear).

12. Where are my keys? They _____ (go)! Did you take them?

13. Mother just called us, because dinner is ready. The table _____ (set),

    the chicken and beans _____ (finish), and the candles

    _____ (light).

14. His room is finally looking cleaner. The bed _____ (make), the floor

    _____ (vacuum), and the windows _____ (wash).

15. We were trapped in a canyon for two days, because the car _____
    (stick) in mud.

16. We are trapped here. The car _____ (stick) in mud.

# The progressive form vs. the stative passive

When the progressive form of *be* is used with past participles, the sentence is in the true passive voice. It is only with the simple conjugation of *be* that a stative passive structure can exist. In addition, a *by* phrase is never used in a stative passive structure. Compare these sets of example sentences.

| | |
|---|---|
| PASSIVE | The roof **is being repaired** by an experienced roofer. |
| STATIVE PASSIVE | The roof **is repaired**. |
| PASSIVE | The children **were being spoiled** by Uncle John. |
| STATIVE PASSIVE | The children **were spoiled**. |
| PASSIVE | The gas **is being turned off** by the repairman. |
| STATIVE PASSIVE | The gas **is turned off**. |

*Complete each sentence, using the appropriate form of be, if needed, and the appropriate form of a verb in the list below.*

| | | | |
|---|---|---|---|
| block | exhaust | marry | stick |
| confuse | go | plug in | turn off |
| crowd | insure | qualify | |
| divorce | locate | schedule | |
| do | lose | spoil | |

1. The meeting _____ for tomorrow at nine.

2. Let's find another bar. This one _____ too _____. It will take us way too long to get a drink.

3. Excuse me. Could you give me directions? I _____.

4. Painting the house is hard work! I don't know how much longer I can help you.

   I _____. We need to rest and just finish up tomorrow.

5. I don't understand the plot of this movie. I thought this was supposed to be a comedy, not a horror movie. I _____.

6. Peter is probably sleeping. The light in his room _____.

7. Her house is very expensive. It _____ for one million dollars.

8. I can't open the garage door. It _____.

9. They were happily married for ten years, but now they _____.

10. I thought I had left my wallet on the table, but it's not there. It _____. I wonder where I could have left it.

11. Mr. Keller, I regret to inform you that you _____ not _____ for the job. We need someone who is more eloquent and organized.

12. I adore Lisa. Every day I think to myself: "I _____ to a wonderful woman."

13. Tell Jamie not to eat that fruit. It _____. Throw it away.

14. I am so tired of having to call the neighbor to move his truck. I am going to be late again for work, because my car _____.

15. St. Thomas _____ in the Virgin Islands.

16. The Internet connection doesn't seem to be working on my computer either. Maybe it's the Ethernet cable. _____ it _____?

17. Sorry, the chicken _____ not _____ yet. I know you're hungry, but you'll have to wait a little longer.

# Prepositions

When certain past participles are used as adjectives in the stative passive, they are often combined with specific prepositions. Following are some frequently used combinations.

accustom – to
acquaint – with
compose – of
cover – with
dedicate – to
devote – to
disappoint – in, with
dress – in
finish – with
interest – in
make – with
marry – to
oppose – to
relate – to
satisfy – with
scare – of
tire – of

When using one of these verbs in the static passive, the appropriate preposition must accompany it.

The bride **is dressed** all **in** white.
I **was tired of** all his complaining.

**EXERCISE**
**11·4**

*Complete each sentence with the correct form of the verb in parentheses plus an appropriate preposition.*

EXAMPLE     A smoothie ___is made with___ fruit juice and ice.  (make)

1. Water _____ hydrogen and oxygen.  (compose)

2. George _____ Greek history.  (interest)

3. He _____ living on his own.  (accustom)

4. My mom _____ large dogs.  (scare)

5. I _____ the progress we have made this past week.  (satisfy)

6. It's autumn, and the country roads _____ leaves.  (cover)

7. We _____ that policy. It's unfair to the immigrant workers.  (oppose)

8. Josh Davis _____ his composition.  (finish)

9. Ruben _____ Eleanor.  (marry)

10. I _____ not _____ that author's work.  (acquaint)

11. She is in a bad mood, because she _____ doing nothing.  (tire)

12. Is your last name really Kennedy? _____ you _____ the Kennedy family? (relate)

13. Steve works for an animal shelter. He _____ his work. (dedicate)

14. The Chicago Bulls lost to a much weaker team. They _____ themselves. (disappoint)

15. I am not as brave as you think. I _____ the noises in my own house. (scare)

16. The administration _____ improving public education. (dedicate)

17. Sarah and I _____ each other. (devote)

18. Marc _____ his best suit for his sister's wedding. (dress)

# Past participles with *get*

Past participles can be used with the verb *get*. *Get* may be followed by a wide variety of adjectives and may occur in any tense, including in a progressive form.

> **I'm getting hungry.** Let's go pick up some food soon.
> I stopped working, because I **got dizzy.**
> You shouldn't eat so much. You **will get fat.**

Following is a list of adjectives commonly used with *get*.

| | | |
|---|---|---|
| angry | dizzy | old |
| anxious | empty | sick |
| bald | (very) far | sleepy |
| better | heavy | tall |
| big | hot | thirsty |
| busy | hungry | warm |
| chilly | late | well |
| cold | mad | wet |
| dark | nervous | worse |

In the structure *get* + past participle, the past participle functions as an adjective; it describes the subject noun or pronoun of the sentence. Consider the following examples.

> They **are getting engaged** next week.
> Dad **got worried,** because Lola was three hours late and didn't bother to call.

Using *get* + past participle instead of *be* + past participle indicates a changing situation. The meaning of *get* in the above sentences is similar to the meaning of *become*. Compare the examples above with the following.

> They **will become engaged** next week.
> Dad **became worried,** because Lola was three hours late and didn't bother to call.

This structure with *get* can occur in any tense.

| | |
|---|---|
| PRESENT | They **get tired.** |
| PRESENT PROGRESSIVE | They **are getting tired** a lot lately. |
| PRESENT PERFECT | They **have gotten tired.** |
| PRESENT PERFECT PROGRESSIVE | They **have been getting tired** a lot lately. |
| PAST | They **got tired.** |
| PAST PROGRESSIVE | They **were getting tired** a lot lately. |
| PAST PERFECT | They **had gotten tired.** |
| PAST PERFECT PROGRESSIVE | They **had been getting tired** a lot lately. |

| FUTURE | They **will get tired**. |
| FUTURE PROGRESSIVE | They **will be getting tired** after just a few minutes of exercise. |
| FUTURE PERFECT | They **will have gotten tired**. |
| FUTURE PERFECT PROGRESSIVE | They **will have been getting tired** after just a few minutes of exercise. |

All the tense forms are grammatically correct. Some, such as the future perfect progressive, are avoided, however, because they sound awkward. A simpler tense is used in place of such awkward phrases.

**EXERCISE**
## 12·1

*Rewrite each sentence with the progressive form of the verb, adding a second clause that provides an interruption of or an explanation for the continuous action. Retain the tense of the original sentence.*

EXAMPLE    She got overtired.

*She was getting overtired, because the heat was so intense.*

1. No one gets hired.

   _____

2. Larry got annoyed.

   _____

3. His pay gets increased.

   _____

4. Younger candidates get elected.

   _____

5. He got fingerprinted.

   _____

**EXERCISE**
## 12·2

*Complete each sentence with an appropriate form of get and the correct form of the verb in parentheses.*

EXAMPLE    The roofers _____*were getting badly sunburned*_____. (badly + sunburn)

1. I think I'll stop jogging. I _____. (tire)

2. When _____ they _____? (marry)

3. We can head out to the discotheque as soon as you _____.
   (dress)

4. He didn't give us proper directions, so we _____. (lost)

5. There was an explosion, but nobody _____. (hurt)

6. I finished painting for today. I _____. (tire)

7. How long did it take her to _____ to living in Boston? (accustom)

8. Sophie said she would call me at eight. It's eleven, and she still hasn't called me, so I _____. (worry)

9. He _____, because everyone told him something different. (confuse)

10. You'll be able to play again. Don't _____ because you lost. (upset)

11. I will meet up with them as soon as I _____. (do)

12. I _____ easily, so I hardly ever finish watching movies. (bore)

13. Peter _____ after losing his job, but now he is doing a little better. (depress)

14. I'll be ready to leave for the airport as soon as I _____. (pack)

15. I _____ on Friday, so that's when I'll buy a new bed. (pay)

16. After Henry graduated from Harvard, he _____ by a large company, but later he _____, because he didn't agree with some of the business policies. (hire/fire)

17. I almost missed the deadline to turn in my thesis. I _____ with my last chapter until four in the morning. (not + finish)

18. First, he _____. Then, he _____. After barely four years, he _____. (engage, marry, divorce)

# ·13· Participial adjectives

Participles, besides being an important element of the progressive forms of tenses (present participles) and of the passive voice (past participles), can also function as adjectives. So far, you have encountered participles in passive structures or as predicate adjectives. But they can also serve as adjectives that modify nouns directly.

## Present participles

Present participles are formed by adding the suffix *-ing* to the base form of the verb (*running, speaking, developing,* and so on). The present participle conveys an active meaning because the noun it modifies is "doing something."

> It is a **confusing** map.  (*The map confuses the driver, because it is not clear.*)
> It is a **boring** story.  (*The story bores the children.*)

## Past participles

Past participles are formed from both regular and irregular verbs. If the verb is regular, the past participle has an *-ed* ending, identical to the simple past-tense form.

> call ~ called
> interest ~ interested
> load ~ loaded
> ship ~ shipped

Irregular verbs form their past participles in a variety of ways. Some have a vowel change in the base form of the word, and many end in *-en*.

> break ~ broken
> see ~ seen
> speak ~ spoken
> take ~ taken

Still others end in *-t*, and many of these have a vowel change as well.

> bring ~ brought
> dream ~ dreamed OR dreamt
> feel ~ felt
> sleep ~ slept

Some participles alter the appearance of the base form only slightly.

> build ~ built
> ran ~ run
> say ~ said

And there are even past participles that are identical to the base form.

> come ~ come
> cut ~ cut
> put ~ put
> shut ~ shut

No matter how they are formed, past participles can be used as modifiers, but with a passive meaning.

> He is a **confused** driver. (*The driver is confused by the map, because it is not clear.*)
> They are **bored** children. (*The children are bored by the story.*)

EXERCISE 13·1

*For each verb, write its present participle and past participle.*

1. sleep _____ _____
2. invent _____ _____
3. lose _____ _____
4. destroy _____ _____
5. compare _____ _____
6. report _____ _____
7. endanger _____ _____
8. make _____ _____
9. steal _____ _____
10. slay _____ _____

Understanding the difference between present participles (active meaning) and past participles (passive meaning) is important in order to form correct sentences with modifiers appropriate to the meaning of the sentences. In the following pairs of examples, compare the difference in meaning of the present participle with that of the past participle.

> John was tearful when he saw what the **damaging** winds had done.
> John was tearful when he saw all the **damaged** homes.

> She observed the **purifying** action of the chemicals on the water.
> She only drinks **purified** water.

*Rewrite each sentence, using the appropriate participial form of the verb in italics—present participle or past participle. Change each sentence according to the example.*

EXAMPLE    The crowd is *amused* by the comedian.

    *They are an amused crowd.*

1. The group of children is *entertained* by the circus clown.

   _____

2. The circus clown *entertains* the kids.

   _____

3. The class *bores* the students.

   _____

4. The students are *bored* by the class.

   _____

5. The accident *frightens* the woman.

   _____

6. The woman was *frightened* by the accident.

   _____

7. The girl was *surprised* by the loud noise.

   _____

8. The loud noise *surprised* the girl.

   _____

9. The hard work *exhausted* the men.

   _____

10. The men were *exhausted*.

   _____

*Complete each sentence with the present or past participle of the verb in parentheses.*

1. The _____ (borrow) tennis racket was returned to the tennis club.

2. The _____ (terrify) civilians ran for their lives.

3. The sudden explosion was a _____ (terrify) sight for the civilians.

4. Success is a _____ (gratify) part of one's work.

5. The _____ (steal) paintings were recovered by the museum.

6. She found herself in an _____ (embarrass) situation this morning.

7. A _____ (damage) hurricane swept across Texas recently.

8. Workers are still in the process of repairing the _____ (damage) streets.

9. I made my way through the _____ (crowd) room.

10. He bought some _____ (freeze) hot dogs at the supermarket.

11. The _____ (injure) cat was taken to the animal shelter.

12. Parents have a _____ (last) effect on their children.

13. I wasn't able to open the _____ (lock) door, so I don't know what's in that room.

14. No one lives in that _____ (desert) mansion. It was abandoned years ago.

# ·14· Subject-verb agreement

Agreement means that two or more words must correspond with each other in order to make proper sense of a sentence. For example, the gender and number of a pronoun or possessive adjective must match the gender and number of the noun it refers to. If you wish to say that a man wants to wear a new shirt he just bought, you would say the following.

> **John** is putting on **his** new shirt.  (MASCULINE SINGULAR SUBJECT /
> MASCULINE SINGULAR POSSESSIVE ADJECTIVE)

That meaning is lost if you change the gender or number of either the subject or the possessive adjective.

> **Mary** is putting on **his** new shirt.
> **John** is putting on **our** new shirt.
> **The boys** are putting on **my** new shirt.

The rules of agreement do not mean that these three examples are incorrect—they could be. But in this case, they are not, because the desired meaning is that a man wants to wear a new shirt he just bought: "He puts on his own shirt."

## Third-person singular and plural

In subject-verb agreement in the third person, the difference between a singular and a plural subject is important. In most cases, a plural subject has a different present-tense verb ending from a singular subject.

> **The boy plays** tag in the street.
> **The boys play** tag in the street.
>
> **She learns** a lot about English.
> **They learn** a lot about English.

When the auxiliary *have* is used in the present perfect tense, there is also a difference between the singular and the plural.

> **My brother has** been in Ireland for two weeks.
> **My parents have** been in Ireland for two weeks.

Using a singular verb with a singular subject and a plural verb with a plural subject is essential for writing and speaking correctly in English.

*Underline the appropriate verb form in each sentence.*

EXAMPLE     There **is** | **are** two magazines on the living room table.

1. There **is** | **are** many reasons for voting.

2. Angela **writes** | **write** lots of e-mails, but she doesn't save any.

3. Peter and I **was** | **were** playing poker the other night.

4. The people in Madrid **is** | **are** very well dressed.

5. Susan's mother always **wakes** | **wake** her up in time for school.

6. My grandmother's friends **likes** | **like** to go to church at noon.

7. There **was** | **were** many children playing in the park.

8. **Does** | **Do** you like those movies?

9. Mother Teresa, Gandhi, and Camus **was** | **were** socially engaged.

10. He **is** | **are** a very good speaker.

---

Subject-verb agreement is essential, no matter what type of verb is involved. When auxiliaries are used, they must be conjugated to agree with the subject of the sentence.

A child **is** playing in the garden.
Many children **are** playing in the park.

**Does** the woman understand English?
**Do** the tourists understand French?

*Complete each sentence with an appropriate form of the verb in parentheses.*

1. They _____ (run) up and down the stairs when the accident took place.

2. My aunt _____ (not + work) in a hair salon.

3. The house _____ (have) a fence around it.

4. Our village's huts _____ (be) exotic.

5. Everybody _____ (scream) really loudly.

# The verb *be*

*Be* is the only English verb that has more than two forms in the simple present tense, which means that agreement involves more than third-person singular and plural forms.

|  | PRESENT SINGULAR | PRESENT PLURAL |
|---|---|---|
| FIRST PERSON | I am | we are |
| SECOND PERSON | you are | you are |
| THIRD PERSON | he/she/it is | they are |

In the past tense, it has two forms.

|  | PAST SINGULAR | PAST PLURAL |
|---|---|---|
| FIRST PERSON | I was | we were |
| SECOND PERSON | you were | you were |
| THIRD PERSON | he/she/it was | they were |

If the subject of the verb *be* is a noun, the third-person form of the verb is used.

**The boy** is at school.
**Mary and Jane** were named co-chairpersons.

---

**EXERCISE**

**14·3**

*Complete each sentence with the appropriate present-tense form of* be.

1. I _____ extremely tired.

2. You _____ very noisy.

3. We _____ from Rwanda.

4. They _____ going to Merida.

5. He _____ a pilot.

6. She _____ always smiling.

7. It _____ a photo of my grandparents.

*Now, complete each sentence with the appropriate past-tense form of* be.

8. I _____ extremely tired.

9. You _____ very noisy.

10. We _____ living in Rwanda.

11. They _____ going to Merida.

12. He _____ a pilot.

13. She _____ always smiling.

14. It _____ a photo that belonged to my grandparents.

15. The barn _____ destroyed during the hurricane.

# Expressions of quantity

For many expressions of quantity, the verb form is determined by the noun or pronoun that follows the word *of*. If the phrase *some of* or *most of* is followed by a singular noun or pronoun, the verb form is singular.

> **Some of** the icing **is** runny.
> **Most of** the equipment **was** sold.

But if these phrases—as well as *many of*—are followed by a plural noun, the verb form is plural.

> **Some of** the movies **are** good.
> **Most of** these people **were** in need of help.
> **Many of** these people **are** my friends.

This concept applies to many other expressions of quantity.

> **One third of** this land **is** mine.
> **Two thirds of** the diamonds **are** mine.
> **A number of** people **miss** the bus.

If *the number* is used instead of *a number* in such an expression, the verb form is singular, because a specific number is being referred to.

> **The number of** people on the bus **is** 52. (*52 **is** the number of people.*)
> **The number of** people at the bar **is** 22. (*22 **is** the number of people.*)

Similarly, expressions with *one of, each of,* and *every one of* take a singular verb form.

> **One of** my parents **is** about to get here.
> **Each one of** my children **is** here.
> **Every one of** my cousins **is** here.

In very formal English, subjects with *none of* are singular, but it is common to hear *none of* used with a plural verb in casual speech.

> FORMAL     **None of** the boys **is** here.
> CASUAL     **None of** the boys **are** here.

**EXERCISE**
## 14·4

*Underline the appropriate verb form in each sentence.*

1. Every one of the soldiers **is** | **are** required to pass the obstacle test.

2. Each girl on the team **has** | **have** her own tennis racket.

3. One of my best friends **is** | **are** suffering from migraines.

4. A lot of shoes on those racks **is** | **are** on sale tomorrow.

5. A lot of women in the class **is** | **are** active feminists.

6. Half of this strawberry cake **belongs** | **belong** to you.

7. Half of the students in this course **is** | **are** from Belgium.

8. Some of the kiwis I bought **is** | **are** really sweet.

9. Some of the fruit I forgot in my car trunk **is** | **are** rotting.

10. Every one of the parts **is** | **are** closely examined for quality control.

11. None of the monkeys at the zoo **is** | **are** free to run away. All of them **is** | **are** locked in small cages.

12. A number of firefighters **is** | **are** off duty today.

13. The number of paintings at the museum **is** | **are** 278.

14. One of the key elements in conflict resolution and peace **is** | **are** honesty.

15. **Does** | **Do** all the children have to take the test?

16. **Does** | **Do** all of his clothes have to be packed by tomorrow?

17. Why **was** | **were** some of the parents pulled aside?

18. Why **was** | **were** the student brought in?

19. **Does** | **Do** any of the workers know where the restaurant is?

20. What part of the human body **is** | **are** most vulnerable?

21. What percentage of the North American population **is** | **are** literate?

---

The expressions *there is* and *there are* are singular and plural, respectively. The noun or pronoun that follows such an expression determines whether the verb is singular or plural.

There **is a man** standing in the parkway.
There **are men** standing in the parkway.
There **is someone** I want you to meet.

---

**EXERCISE**
**14·5**

*Underline the appropriate verb form in each sentence.*

1. There **is** | **are** hundreds of types of tea in China.

2. There **is** | **are** a mosquito in my tent!

3. There **is** | **are** many ways to get downtown.

4. There **isn't** | **aren't** a message for you.

5. There **is** | **are** a report on the incident.

6. There **isn't** | **aren't** laws against free speech.

7. How many kinds of frogs **is** | **are** there in South America?

8. Why **isn't** | **aren't** there a public school in town?

9. There **is** | **are** a ruler in my bag.

10. There **is** | **are** some erasers and highlighters in my drawer.

# Collective nouns

Occasionally, a noun ending in -*s* is singular. This is especially true of collective nouns and noun phrases that are considered indivisible units.

> The United States **is** an important country.
> The news **is** televised.
> The Maldives **consists** of 26 atolls.
> The United Nations **has** five principal administrative bodies.
> Macy's **is** a department store.
> Physics **is** a science.

Note that if such a noun is changed to a pronoun, the singular pronoun *it* is used. This is because the noun is considered singular: *The United Nations* is one unit and is therefore replaced by *it* and not by *they* or *them*.

This same concept can be applied to expressions of **time**, **distance**, and **money**.

> **Ten hours** of flying **is** too long.
> **Thirty miles is** the exact distance from here to there.
> **Fifty dollars is** too expensive.

Note, however, that the nouns *people* and *police* are plural and take plural verb forms.

> **All those people are** trapped inside their homes.
> **The police have** intervened swiftly.

Finally, there are several adjectives preceded by *the* that are used as **plural nouns**.

> **The old are** not well taken care of in this country.
> **The rich keep** getting richer.
> **The wrongly accused deserve** justice.
> **The injured and wounded lie** about the battlefield.

Following is a list of other adjectives that are used as plural nouns.

> the blind
> the dead
> the deaf
> the handicapped
> the living
> the young

**EXERCISE**

**14·6**

*Underline the appropriate verb form in each sentence.*

1. Ten dollars **is** | **are** a reasonable price for an ink pen.

2. Five minutes **is** | **are** all the time allocated for the exam.

3. The number on that car's license plate **is** | **are** fake.

4. Mathematics **is** | **are** used to calculate everything.

5. Physics **tries** | **try** to explain motion.

6. Massachusetts **is** | **are** 200 miles away from the border.

7. The news about the plane crash **is** | **are** pretty alarming.

8. The United Nations **is** | **are** an important international institution.

9. Many people in the world **does** | **do** not own a home.

10. The police **is** | **are** paid for by tax money and federal funds.

11. Many Japanese people **likes** | **like** pop culture.

12. Portuguese **is** | **are** similar to Spanish in pronunciation.

13. In horror movies, the living **fears** | **fear** the dead.

14. Most people **is** | **are** not allergic to bee stings.

15. The effect of the volcano's eruption **depends** | **depend** on how elevated it is.

16. There **has** | **have** been some cases of bubonic plague in the south of the island.

---

EXERCISE
14·7

*Complete each sentence with the correct simple present form of the verb in parentheses.*

EXAMPLE _____*Are*_____ (be) Ben and Tina excited about going to the movies?

1. _____ (be) July and August the hottest months of the year in Houston?

2. The interest rates for the house loan _____ (be) cheap, because it is a small house.

3. A blue parrot and a yellow parrot _____ (be) perched in the cage.

4. A yellow and blue car _____ (be) parked in the driveway.

5. _____ (do) most of the children take a nap after lunch?

6. _____ (do) John's dog always bark that loudly?

7. My spare key _____ (be) in my back pocket.

8. Each dollar, quarter, dime, and cent _____ (be) carefully accounted for in our company.

9. Attentiveness to other people's reactions _____ (make) an efficient salesman.

10. One of my sisters _____ (keep) a hairbrush in her purse at all times.

11. There _____ (be) lots of horses competing in the race this year.

12. My neighbor _____ (knock) on my door every morning at seven to wake me up.

13. Almost one third of the land in the southwestern part of Montgomery County

    _____ (be) unsuitable for growing crops.

14. The economic and social center of the United States _____ (be) New York.

15. Three hours of jogging _____ (provide) plenty of exercise.

16. In many ways, the proposed constitutional amendment on digital information
    _____ (violate) freedom of speech.

17. A bicycle with no visible lights and no brakes _____ (be) dangerous.

18. A number of parents from the association _____ (plan) to protest.

19. Most of the news on the front page of the *New York Times* _____ (be) about the
    explosion that took place at the Jordanian embassy.

20. The number of Aztec artifacts found in the pyramid _____ (be) 20.

21. Almost all of the historical records on the Carter family _____ (be) fake.

22. Every day, there _____ (be) more than 200 babies born in Missouri.

23. No news _____ (be) good news.

24. Every member of this group _____ (be) quite intelligent.

# Auxiliary verbs

If a verb phrase contains an auxiliary verb, it is the auxiliary verb, and no other verbal element, that must agree with the subject of the sentence. Examples with the auxiliary *be* follow.

| SINGULAR | PLURAL |
| --- | --- |
| he is singing | they are singing |
| he is punished | they are punished |
| he is used to it | they are used to it |
| he is to be freed | they are to be freed |
| he was speaking | they were speaking |
| he was found guilty | they were found guilty |

Examples with the auxiliary *have* follow.

| SINGULAR | PLURAL |
| --- | --- |
| he has learned | they have learned |
| he has been jogging | they have been jogging |
| he has been arrested | they have been arrested |
| he had been hurrying | they had been hurrying |

Examples with the auxiliary *do* follow.

| SINGULAR | PLURAL |
| --- | --- |
| Does he understand? | Do they understand? |
| He does not understand. | They do not understand. |
| He did not care. | They did not care. |

No matter how complicated the verb phrase is, only the auxiliary verb form agrees with the subject of the sentence. The other elements of the phrase remain the same.

# Complex sentences

A dependent clause is called a relative clause when it begins with *who, which,* or *that.* When one of these words is immediately followed by a verb phrase, the relative pronoun (*who, which, that*) becomes the subject of the clause. Consider the following examples.

The man, **who** was walking down the street, was poor.
Peter usually eats macaroni and cheese, **which** is his favorite dish.
Do you see the plane **that** is flying away?

If *who, which,* or *that* is the subject of the relative clause, the verb must reflect the number of that subject: singular or plural. If the antecedent of *who, which,* or *that* is singular, the relative pronoun is singular. If the antecedent is plural, the relative pronoun is plural. And in both instances, the verb will agree with the number of the antecedent and relative pronoun.

SINGULAR ANTECEDENT

The **boy**, who is throwing stones, is going to break a window.
The **car**, which is being built in Detroit, has GPS as a standard feature.
John found a **pen** that is made of silver.

PLURAL ANTECEDENT

The **boys**, who are throwing stones, are going to break a window.
The **cars**, which are being built in Detroit, have GPS as a standard feature.
Mary found two **pens** that are made of silver.

While *who, which,* or *that* can be the subject of the relative clause, *whose* cannot be a subject. In this case, the subject of the clause is the noun that immediately follows *whose.*

He is the architect **whose mother** comes from a poor country.

In this sentence, the subject of the relative clause is *mother* and the verb is *comes,* the third-person singular form that agrees with the singular noun *mother.* It is possible for *whose* to be used with a plural subject.

He is the architect **whose parents** come from a poor country.

## EXERCISE
## 14·8

*Underline the antecedent(s) of* who, which, *or* that *in each sentence.*

1. Frank plays tennis with Mark and Pamela, who are his best friends.

2. She works in Manhattan, which is the most densely populated borough in New York City.

3. People who live in a house are fortunate.

4. Do you see the cars that are parked at the end of this street?

*Underline the appropriate verb form in each sentence.*

1. The book that **was** | **were** on the table is mine.

2. Tyler, who **is** | **are** already finished with law school, is 22 years old.

3. Tour guides who **talks** | **talk** too much are annoying.

4. The government must support people who **is** | **are** poor.

5. Sophie ate the brownies that **was** | **were** on the plate.

# Agreement with nouns

Pronouns replace nouns in a sentence. Like nouns, pronouns can act as the subject or the object of a sentence. A singular pronoun is used to replace a singular noun.

> **A boy** ran into the living room. **He** was looking for his toy.
> Did you see **the boy** come in? Did you see **him** come in?

A plural pronoun is used to replace a plural noun.

> **Some children** ran out to the garden. **They** were looking for Easter eggs.
> They gave candy to **some children.** They gave candy to **them.**

## Personal pronouns and collective nouns

When a **collective noun** refers to a single, impersonal entity, a singular pronoun (such as *it*) is used.

> **My work team** is large. **It** is composed of 20 analysts.

When a collective noun refers to a group of various individuals, a plural pronoun (such as *they* or *them*) is used.

> **That family** is close and caring. **They** are always there to support each other.

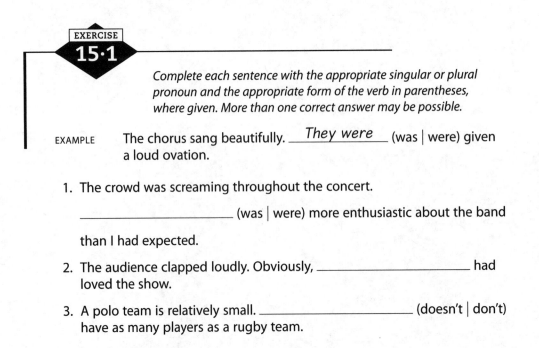

EXERCISE
15·1

*Complete each sentence with the appropriate singular or plural pronoun and the appropriate form of the verb in parentheses, where given. More than one correct answer may be possible.*

EXAMPLE    The chorus sang beautifully. ___*They were*___ (was | were) given a loud ovation.

1. The crowd was screaming throughout the concert.

    _____ (was | were) more enthusiastic about the band

    than I had expected.

2. The audience clapped loudly. Obviously, _____ had loved the show.

3. A polo team is relatively small. _____ (doesn't | don't) have as many players as a rugby team.

4. The basketball team felt discouraged, because _____ had lost to the opposing team.

5. I wrote a story on the average American family. During my research, I found out that

   _____ (is | are) composed of about two children.

6. I have a wonderful group of co-workers. I enjoy working with _____

   very much, and _____ (appreciates | appreciate) my work.

7. The fans became more and more excited as the game progressed.

   _____ began to chant and wave flags in the air.

8. The audience at the Philip Glass concert was huge. _____ exceeded 20,000 people.

9. The marketing team is pretty large. _____ (consists | consist) of 32 research specialists, 5 accountants, 10 secretaries, and 2 managers.

10. Martha and David finally saved enough money to begin making payments on the new car

    _____ bought.

11. The research team is planning a trip to southern Mexico. _____ (is | are) going to have fun.

12. There aren't enough people registered for the course. _____ (is | are) probably going to be canceled.

## Noncount nouns

There is a group of English nouns that are neither singular nor plural and cannot be counted. These nouns are referred to as **noncount nouns**.

The rule for using them is quite simple: When used as the subject of a sentence, a noncount noun takes the third-person singular form of the verb.

> The water tastes funny.
> Sunshine makes me happy.

A noncount noun cannot be used with the indefinite article *a/an*, which means "one." Compare the following sentences.

> CORRECT    I drank **the water**.
> CORRECT    I drank **water**.
> INCORRECT  I drank **a water**.

Because it has an uncertain volume, *water* is a noncount noun. Therefore, the word *a* cannot be used in the third sentence above, because water cannot be counted and is neither singular nor plural. Following are examples of other noncount nouns used in sentences.

> My professor gives us **homework**.
> They borrowed **furniture**.
> I have **time** to do the dishes.
> We had **money** back then.
> Los Angeles has **traffic** day and night.
> She didn't get **mail**.

He wears **jewelry**.
Bruno sold **clothes**.

If a noun makes no sense when preceded by *a/an,* it is a noncount noun. However, certain other words can be used to specify an indefinite quantity with this category of nouns, such as *some, little, a lot of,* and *much.*

He bought **some** jewelry in an antique store.
I have **little** time for this.
Do they have **a lot of** money?
There's too **much** furniture in this room.

A list of other common noncount nouns follows.

| | | | |
|---|---|---|---|
| anger | economics | honesty | rice |
| biology | electricity | humidity | salt |
| bread | experience | love | silver |
| cement | fire | luck | snow |
| chalk | fog | meat | sugar |
| cotton | food | peace | violence |
| courage | gold | plastic | wheat |
| darkness | grass | poverty | wind |
| dirt | gravity | progress | wood |
| dust | heat | rain | wool |

Some of these nouns can also be used with *a/an* when they are specific in meaning and not used to express the general meaning of the noun.

| SPECIFIC MEANING | GENERAL MEANING |
|---|---|
| an **experience** I'll never forget | **Experience** is the best teacher. |
| a **fire** of catastrophic proportions | **Fire** is so destructive. |
| a **love** of raw nature | I just want **love**. |
| a lasting **peace** | May you live in **peace**. |
| a **silver** of exceptional purity | There is **silver** in this mine. |

EXERCISE
15·2

*Fill in the blank after each expression of quantity with an appropriate noun. If both a regular noun and a collective noun can be used with the quantity, give an example of each.*

EXAMPLE    a lot of ___*problems / time*___

1. a few _____

2. many _____

3. several _____

4. some _____

5. a little _____

6. six _____

7. much _____

8. little _____

**EXERCISE**
**15·3**

*Underline the verb form that correctly completes each sentence.*

1. The problem **is** | **are** that oil has become too expensive in the last few years.

2. I find that the homework **is** | **are** usually too easy.

3. You should be certain that the water **is** | **are** drinkable.

4. I will feel more secure if her money **stays** | **stay** in the bank.

5. When I saw that my clothing **was** | **were** so white, I was happy with the cleaning service.

**EXERCISE**
**15·4**

*Underline the word or phrase that correctly completes each sentence.*

1. The new puppy has brought me **much** | **many** happiness.

2. Jerusalem is like other major cities that have **much** | **many** traffic.

3. Last night at the party, I met **a little** | **some** people who spoke French.

4. Cuba is great. There are many beaches to discover, and there **is** | **are** plenty of entertainment.

5. Reading is good. I have gotten **much** | **many** knowledge from books, and I have learned about all sorts of things.

6. I bought four **bread** | **loaves** at the supermarket.

7. Even after paying for the movie rental, he still had **a few** | **a little** money to spend.

8. They are among **the few** | **much** people to have survived.

9. I think it is rather strange that we don't hear **much** | **many** news from them anymore.

10. We have all probably made **a little** | **a few** progress in English spelling.

# Indefinite pronouns

In formal English, a singular personal pronoun or possessive adjective is used to refer to an **indefinite pronoun**. Indefinite pronouns are those that do not refer to a specific person, for example, *anybody, somebody,* and *everyone.*

> **Somebody** left **his/her** keys on the counter.
> **Everyone** has **his/her** own way of doing things.

In informal English, a plural personal pronoun is often used to refer to an indefinite pronoun.

> **Somebody** left **their** keys on the counter.
> **Everyone** has **their** own way of doing things.

Following is a list of the most common indefinite pronouns.

anybody
anyone
anything

everybody
everyone
everything

nobody
no one
nothing

somebody
someone
something

EXERCISE

**15·5**

*Underline the verb form that correctly completes each sentence.*

1. Something **was** | **were** making scary noises up in the attic.

2. The police spoke to each person who **was** | **were** at the crime scene.

3. Almost every student who **studies** | **study** at the library gets more work done.

4. Nobody from the crime scene **wants** | **want** to answer the policewoman's questions.

5. Someone **is** | **are** responsible for this error.

6. Almost everybody in my office **drinks** | **drink** coffee in the morning.

EXERCISE

**15·6**

*Fill in the blank with an appropriate pronoun or possessive adjective. If a choice of verbs is provided, write in the correct one. More than one correct answer may be possible.*

EXAMPLE     When an artist wants to paint, ___*she*___ should try to find inspiration.

1. Anyone can learn how to play guitar if _____ (wants | want) to.

2. Doctors diagnose patients, but _____ (is | are) not allowed to operate
   on you if they are not trained.

3. Each player on our soccer team has to spend three hours a day lifting weights,

   a process during which _____ (builds | build) stamina following the directions

   of _____ trainer.

4. A politician has two primary responsibilities. _____ should respect the popular

   vote, and _____ should avoid war at all costs.

5. If Alex wants to read, _____ should try to find a quiet place.

6. Someone forgot _____ jacket. I wonder who it belongs to.

7. Everyone who came to the party brought _____ own drink.

8. I wonder whose book this is. I should look inside the front cover to check if

_____ wrote _____ name or phone number.

9. A dog can do cool tricks if _____ (is | are) taken care of and properly trained.

10. John's hamster is called Wooblee Beeboo. _____ (is | are) very noisy.

_____ recognizes John only if _____ notices that John has food

in _____ hand.

# Complex nouns

**Complex nouns** are phrases that combine a head noun with a subordinate noun. The **head noun** is the subject of the sentence and determines the form of the verb. The **subordinate noun** is the object of the preposition *of*; the *of* phrase follows the head noun and completes the meaning of the subject. The phrase *the glasses of wine* consists of the head noun *glasses*, the preposition *of*, and the subordinate noun *wine*.

> **The glasses of wine** are on the bar.

A plural verb (*are*) is required in this sentence, because the subject (*glasses*) is plural. If the noun phrase has a singular subject, the verb form is singular.

> **A bottle of wine** is in the cooler.

**EXERCISE 15·7**

*Fill in the blank with a verb form or expression of quantity that makes sense.*

EXAMPLES     Each of the boys ___*has*___ been given a dollar.

Chicago has ___*many*___ kinds of ethnic neighborhoods.

1. The cans of food _____ in the trunk.

2. One of the students _____ studying.

3. Ten loaves of bread _____ needed to make the sandwiches.

4. There _____ several types of entertainment in Madagascar.

5. My sister doesn't drink _____ cups of coffee in the afternoon, because it keeps her awake at night.

6. That _____ an unexpected piece of news.

7. Large avenues have _____ lanes to clear out traffic.

# ·16· Using *other*

Forms of *other* are used as either adjectives or pronouns. These forms distinguish singular from plural, both as adjectives and pronouns.

## Adjectives

The adjective *another* is used to modify singular nouns. Its plural counterpart, *other,* is used to modify plural nouns, noncount nouns, and collective nouns. *Another* means "one more of something" or "something different." *Other* means "more things or persons" or "different things or persons."

> I want **another** piece of cake, please.  (*one more*)
> I don't like this apple. I'd prefer **another** apple.  (*a different one*)
>
> We met the **other** guests at the party.  (*more of them*)
> They're strange. I'd rather meet the **other** guests.  (*different ones*)
> Some books were interesting. **Other** books were quite boring.
>     (*different ones*)
> I like this wine, but I think the **other** wine is better.  (*different noncount*)

*Other* and *the other* can modify plural nouns. They are different only in that *the other* is more specific. But be aware that *the other* can also modify singular nouns.

> Some plants are wilted. **Other** plants seem to be thriving.
>     (*plural, others in general*)
> These trees need to be sprayed. **The other** trees look healthy.
>     (*plural, specific others*)
> This rose bush needs trimming. **The other** rose bush is perfect.  (*singular*)

*Another* is also used with expressions of money, time, and distance; in these cases, it means "an additional." Even though many of these expressions are plural, *another* is the appropriate modifier.

> This is not enough. We need **another** hundred euros.
> She will live in this house for **another** six weeks.
> They had to walk **another** five miles to get here.

*Every other* indicates alternating items in a series, for example, counting by even numbers: *two, four, six, eight,* and so on.

> Please respond to **every other** question.  (*numbers one, three, five, seven*)
> I speak to my brother **every other** day.  (*Monday, Wednesday, Friday*)

*Fill in the blank with an appropriate noun phrase.*

EXAMPLE     another ___*meeting of the board of directors*___

1. another _____
2. another _____
3. another _____
4. another _____
5. other _____
6. other _____
7. other _____
8. other _____

# Pronouns

The pronominal form of *another* is *another* or *another one*. It replaces a phrase in which the adjective *another* modifies a singular noun. If *the other* is used to modify a singular noun, it changes to *the other one* when the noun is replaced.

| | |
|---|---|
| Do you want **another** cup of coffee? | Do you want **another**? |
| I can't deal with **another** problem. | I can't deal with **another one**. |
| Give the boy **another** quarter. | Give the boy **another one**. |
| **The other** novel is far better. | **The other one** is far better. |

The pronominal form of *other* is *others*. It replaces a phrase in which the adjective *other* modifies a plural noun.

Some tourists brought cameras. **Others** just bought postcards of the scene.
Many people are worried about the problem. **Others** just don't care.

To be more specific, *the others* is used.

A few runners made it to the finish. **The others** dropped out an hour ago.
Some of the guests got drunk. **The others** just watched them in amusement.

The following example sentences illustrate various uses of the forms of *other*.

One conference speaker is from California. **Another** speaker is from Boston.
**Other** speakers are from Chicago. Still **others** are from New York.
I have four Lou Reed records. Three are mine, and I bought them last week. **The other** record is his. But I only have three David Bowie records. The one with the psychedelic cover is mine. **The other** records are yours.

*Each other* and *one another* express reciprocity.

We e-mail **each other** every morning.
We write to **one another** every afternoon.

Complete each sentence with an appropriate form of other.

EXAMPLE     Take these two shirts. This one is for your mom, and ___the other___ is for your dad.

1. This cookie is for you, and _____ one is for my sister.

2. There are many modes of transportation. The bus is one way. _____ are the car, the bicycle, and the motorcycle.

3. I would like to write more about this topic. Do you have _____ book I could borrow from you to learn more about it?

4. I would like some more books on the topic. Do you have any _____ that you could lend me?

5. She invited three people over for dinner. Of those three people, only Marie and Sebastian can come. _____ person can't come.

6. Look at your feet. One is your right foot, and _____ is your left foot.

7. Look at your hand. You have five fingers. One is your pinky. _____ is your ring finger. _____ is your middle finger. _____ finger is your index finger. And _____ is your thumb.

8. I got three e-mails. One was from my aunt. _____ one was from my girlfriend, who is studying in Korea. _____ e-mail was from my friend Tyler.

9. There are two children sitting at the bus stop. One is Christopher, and _____ is Richard, my son.

10. Monica reads *The Economist* every week. She doesn't read any _____ magazine.

11. Some people prefer hip-hop, but _____ prefer rap music.

12. Mr. and Mrs. Kuichi are a happily married couple. They respect _____. They support _____. They enjoy being with _____.

13. She will graduate in _____ two years.

14. I'm almost done. I just need _____ two hours.

15. There are two ways to get to the island. The plane is one means of transportation. The boat is _____.

16. The country has two basic problems. One is corruption, and _____ is rampant inflation.

17. Some people are loud; _____ are quiet. Some people are outspoken; _____ are shy. Some people are smart; _____ are not so smart.

18. Most of the children have arrived, and I am sure _____ will be here soon.

19. Thank you for inviting me to go swimming. I'd really like to accept, but I already have

_____ plans.

20. They have three girls. One of them is in high school and still has _____ year

to go before she graduates. _____ is about to go to college.

_____ is about to finish her doctorate.

21. One of the countries I'd like to visit is Hungary. _____ is Russia. Of course,

besides those two countries, there are many _____ I'd like to visit.

22. Three countries border Spain. One is France. _____ is Portugal.

_____ is Andorra.

23. I have been to only three cities since I came to Italy. One is Rome, and

_____ are Turin and Florence.

24. When his alarm rang in the morning, he hit the snooze button, closed his eyes, and went

back to sleep for _____ ten minutes.

25. Patrick and I have been friends for a long time. We've known _____ since
we were kids.

26. It's a long drive. I'm already tired of being in the car, and we still have _____
800 miles to go.

27. Prices continually rise. Next year, a pound of fruit will cost _____ three
or four dollars more than it does now.

# Gerunds

**Gerunds** are verb forms that function as nouns. They are formed by adding the suffix *-ing* to the base form of the verb: *talking, running, building, developing,* and so on.

Gerunds can function as subjects or objects.

GERUND AS SUBJECT

**Working** has never been John's strong point.
**Swimming** is really great exercise.

GERUND AS OBJECT

I enjoy **working** at the plant, but I prefer **gardening**.
She always liked **knitting** and has made a good business out of it.

EXERCISE
**17·1**

*Complete each sentence with an appropriate gerund.*

EXAMPLES    I don't care for ___*boating*___ .

I don't care for ___*dancing*___ .

1. My sister never liked _____ .

   My sister never liked _____ .

   My sister never liked _____ .

   My sister never liked _____ .

2. The boys were interested in _____ .

   The boys were interested in _____ .

   The boys were interested in _____ .

   The boys were interested in _____ .

# Distinguishing gerunds from present participles

Although gerunds look like present participles, they function in a different way. Present participles are typically part of a progressive verb phrase and follow the auxiliary verb *be*. Gerunds are only used as nouns.

PRESENT PARTICIPLES

She **was cooking** and **cleaning** all day long.  (PAST PROGRESSIVE)
Tom and Marie **have been jogging** for over an hour.  (PRESENT PERFECT PROGRESSIVE)

GERUNDS

**Jogging** is always healthy.  (SUBJECT)
Dad had to do the **cooking** and **cleaning** by himself.  (DIRECT OBJECT)

# The possessive

In formal English, a noun or pronoun preceding a gerund is in the form of a possessive.

We appreciated **Tara's** letting us use her phone.
I never liked **his** dating that girl.

In casual English, however, an object form of a noun or pronoun quite commonly precedes a gerund.

We appreciated **Tara** letting us use her phone.
I never liked **him** dating that girl.

Although the direct object + gerund construction is heard with great frequency, the possessive construction is preferred.

I was very annoyed by **William's** driving so recklessly.
We were all so proud of **Linda's** winning the race.
I couldn't bear the **child's** crying.
Julian's sister did not approve of **his** drinking.
They all hated **my** singing and especially **my** dancing.

A word of caution: If a verb form ending in *-ing* precedes a noun, the verb form is a present participle, because its function in that position is as a modifier of the noun.

The other soldiers were distracted by William's **twitching muscles**.
They all hated his **reverberating baritone**.

EXERCISE
17·2

*Underline the gerund(s) in each sentence.*

1. Moving to a new city is always stressful.

2. Mentioning this to Paul would be very clumsy.

3. She is looking forward to meeting him in person.

4. Managing this store is becoming too overwhelming.

5. We enjoy walking in the countryside and swimming in rivers.

*Fill in the blank with the appropriate gerund form of the verb in parentheses.*

1. They warned me that _____ (reach) the top of the mountain would take several days.

2. _____ (Decide) where to keep our old winter boots was not too difficult.

3. The policeman's job is _____ (protect) citizens and _____ (serve) the law.

4. Laura does not seem to have time to do anything but _____ (study) and _____ (stay) out late with her friends.

5. I made a living by _____ (paint) houses and _____ (repair) roofs.

6. Rehearse _____ (sing) that song with your professor; otherwise, you'll never get better.

7. She cannot ask her parents to keep her dog without _____ (alert) them to her vacation plans.

8. _____ (Listen) to Paco de Lucía playing acoustic guitar was amazing.

9. _____ (Stretch) has always been my favorite form of relaxation.

10. _____ (Rhyme) and _____ (dance) are crucial elements of hip-hop culture.

# Conjunctions

Conjunctions connect words, phrases, and clauses. But not all conjunctions function in the same way. This unit describes the types of English conjunctions and how they are used in sentences.

## Coordinating conjunctions

**Coordinating conjunctions** connect words or groups of words of the same grammatical type, such as verbs, nouns, and adjectives, or of the same grammatical structure, such as phrases and clauses. These are the coordinating conjunctions: *and, but, or, yet, for, so,* and *nor.*

If a coordinating conjunction connects more than two elements, it is generally placed between the last two elements of the series. The other elements are separated by commas.

> In order to find the treasure, you will need a compass, a shovel, a map, **and** a lamp.
> He wanted to buy a hat, a pair of gloves, **or** some new boots.

Coordinating conjunctions can also connect other elements, such as infinitives and infinitive phrases.

> She wants to watch a movie **or** (to) listen to music.
> It's difficult to listen to him **and** to know that he is lying.

If a coordinating conjunction connects independent clauses, the conjunction is usually preceded by a comma. An independent clause is one that can stand by itself and make complete sense. If a coordinating conjunction connects independent clauses, it creates a **compound sentence**.

> She spoke to him harshly, **but** there was real pity for him in her heart.
> Tom was exhausted, **yet** he found enough strength to lead them out of the woods.

If the subject, verb, or auxiliary is the same in both clauses, the one in the second clause can be omitted. When this occurs, the comma can be omitted.

> He spoke slowly **but** [he] pronounced each word in anger.
> The men worked on the house **and** [worked] on the shed in the backyard.
> Someone is knocking at the door **and** [is] calling your name.

# Conjunctions and their meaning

*But* and *yet* indicate a contrast between the elements they connect.

His knee was hurting, **but** he finished the race anyway.
The grape juice was bitter **yet** hydrating.

*Or* indicates a choice or offers alternatives between the elements it connects.

On Sunday, we will go to the lake **or** to the river.
He wants a new bicycle **or** some roller skates for Christmas.

*Nor* typically connects negative statements. Note that if an independent clause follows *nor*, its subject and verb are inverted.

They did not fix my camera, **nor** did they fix my lens.
She did not tell us where she was traveling to, **nor** did she tell us how long she would be gone.

The conjunction *for* is generally synonymous with *because*. *So* has a meaning similar to *therefore*. *For* and *so* can also express a cause-and-effect relationship.

She could not think clearly, **for** her heart was so full of anger.
They could not find the car keys, **so** they broke the window to get in.

---

### EXERCISE
### 18·1

*Fill in the blank with an appropriate word or words. Then, combine each group of sentences into one sentence, using a coordinating conjunction. Use appropriate punctuation.*

EXAMPLE  The concert was crowded. The concert was loud. The concert was ___*fun*___.
  *The concert was crowded, loud, and fun.*

1. The car was small. The car was dirty. The car was _____.

   _____

2. The country lane was narrow. The country lane was long. The country lane was

   _____.

   _____

3. I dislike living downtown because of the noise. I dislike living downtown because of the

   crime. I dislike living downtown because of the _____.

   _____

4. The Dominican Republic has _____. The Dominican Republic has palm trees.
   The Dominican Republic has pretty beaches. The Dominican Republic has tropical birds.

   _____

   _____

   _____

5. I like to become acquainted with people from other countries. I like to become acquainted with customs from other countries. I like to become acquainted with _____ from other countries.

_____

_____

EXERCISE
18·2

*Combine each group of sentences into one sentence, using a coordinating conjunction. Remember that using a coordinating conjunction allows you to omit repeated words.*

EXAMPLE        Peter is staying home. Peter is sleeping.
               *Peter is staying home and sleeping.*

1. Susan washed the dishes. Susan put the food away.

_____

2. Peter opened the door. Peter greeted the guests.

_____

3. Ralph is painting the garage door. Ralph is cleaning the brushes.

_____

4. Simon is generous. Simon is handsome. Simon is intelligent.

_____

5. Please try to make less noise. Please try to have some respect for others.

_____

6. She gave him chocolates on Monday. She gave him a CD on Tuesday. She gave him a bracelet on Wednesday.

_____

7. While we were in Los Angeles, we went to a concert. While we were in Los Angeles, we ate Mexican food. While we were in Los Angeles, we visited old friends.

_____

_____

8. I should have finished my project. I should have cleaned my car.

_____

9. He preferred to play poker. Sometimes he preferred to spend time in museums.

_____

10. I like water. I don't like soda.

_____

*Complete each sentence with the appropriate coordinating conjunction.*

1. Jean-Paul Sartre wrote theatrical plays _____ literary essays.

2. The water levels were rising, _____ we had to climb on top of the roof.

3. She is beautiful, _____ her personality is cold.

4. You must wear a jacket in Boston in the winter, _____ you will catch a cold.

5. They asked us to come in, _____ we said no.

6. John did not have money, _____ did Barbara.

7. Patrick _____ Rebecca were standing in the living room.

8. She went downstairs _____ opened the door.

# Correlative conjunctions

**Correlative conjunctions** follow the same set of rules coordinating conjunctions do. Both types of conjunctions function in the same way, except that correlative conjunctions are composed of two parts. The most common of these conjunctions are *both . . . and . . .*, *not only . . . but also . . .*, *either . . . or . . .*, and *neither . . . nor . . .*.

When two subjects are connected by *not only . . . but also . . .*, *either . . . or . . .*, or *neither . . . nor . . .*, the subject that is closer to the verb determines whether the verb is singular or plural. However, when two subjects are connected with *both . . . and . . .*, the verb is always plural.

> **Not only** my sister **but also** my cousin is here.
> **Not only** my sister **but also** my parents are here.
>
> **Either** the cops **or** the robber was blamed for the victim's death.
> **Either** my sister **or** my parents were in attendance.
>
> **Neither** my sister **nor** my cousin is here.
> **Neither** my sister **nor** my parents are here.
>
> **Both** my sister **and** my cousin are here.
> **Both** the winter **and** the spring have been cold and damp.

These examples illustrate correlative conjunctions used with the subjects of the sentences. They can also be used to join objects in a sentence.

> He teased **both** my sister **and** my cousin.
> She bought **not only** a new blouse **but also** a new skirt.
> I spoke to **either** your wife **or** your daughter.
> We saw **neither** the crime **nor** the criminal.

*Complete each sentence with* is *or* are.

1. Both the coach and the player _____ present.

2. Neither the coach nor the player _____ present.

3. Not only the coach but also the players _____ present.

4. Not only the coach but also the player _____ present.

5. Either the players or the coach _____ using the weight room.

6. Either the coach or the players _____ using the weight room.

EXERCISE
18·5

*Combine each pair of sentences into one sentence, using a correlative conjunction.*

1. She does not have a pen. She does not have a ruler.

   _____

2. The giant panda faces extinction. The white tiger faces extinction.

   _____

3. We could drive. We could take the bus.

   _____

4. She wants to buy a Honda. She wants to buy a Toyota.

   _____

5. We can fix dinner for them at home. We can take them to a restaurant.

   _____

6. Joseph is absent. Peter is absent.

   _____

7. Joe is not in class today. Pedro is not in class today.

   _____

8. You can have tea. You can have coffee.

   _____

9. Roger enjoys playing Nintendo. Sam enjoys playing Nintendo.

   _____

10. The President's press secretary will not confirm the story. The President's press secretary
    will not deny the story.

   _____

11. Coal is a nonrenewable natural resource. Petroleum is a nonrenewable natural resource.

_____

12. Bird flu is a dangerous disease. Malaria is a dangerous disease.

_____

13. Her parents don't know where she is. Her boyfriend doesn't know where she is.

_____

14. According to the weather report, it will rain tomorrow. It will be windy tomorrow.

_____

*Underline the conjunction(s) in each sentence.*

1. He did not know whether he was on the right street or completely lost, for night was coming and the streets were getting dark.

2. She was hungry and wanted either a cup of water or a glass of lemonade.

3. The movie was not only interesting but beautiful, and it inspired me.

4. Neither argument nor begging would change the jury's verdict, but the defendant appealed the case.

5. Both the teacher and the students were eager to see the play, but unfortunately it was sold out.

Complete sentences are separated by a period, not a comma.

> It was very cold. He put on a sweater.
> We borrowed some money. We bought a used car.

However, you can use a comma before a coordinating conjunction to combine two sentences into a single sentence. If the subjects of the two sentences are identical, the subject of the second sentence can be omitted. In such a case, the comma is not used.

> It was very cold, **and** he put on a sweater.
> We borrowed money **and** bought a used car.

If the sentences are very short, the comma can be omitted.

> The concert ended **and** he left.

*Punctuate the following sentences, adding commas and periods and capitalizing letters where necessary. If a sentence needs no changes, mark it with an X.*

1. The men walked the boys ran.

2. Sylvia came to the meeting her brother stayed home.

3. Sylvia came to the meeting but her brother stayed home.

4. The professor spoke and the students listened.

5. The professor spoke the students listened.

6. His academic record was outstanding yet he was not accepted into Harvard.

7. Her academic record was outstanding she was not accepted into Harvard but she was not too unhappy about it.

8. We had to go to the grocery store for some milk and bread.

9. We had to go to the grocery store for there was nothing to eat in the fridge.

10. A barometer measures air pressure a thermometer measures temperature.

11. The Egyptians had good sculptors archeologists have found marvelous statues buried in the pyramids.

12. Murdock made many promises but he had no intention of keeping them he was known to be a liar.

13. I always enjoyed studying geography in high school so I decided to pursue it in college.

14. Cecilia is in serious legal trouble for she had no car insurance at the time of the accident.

15. Last night, Marie had to study for an exam so she went to a coffeehouse.

16. The team of scientists has not finished analyzing the virus yet their work will not be published until later this year.

17. You have nothing to fear for they are strong and united.

18. She threw the book out the window she had failed the exam again so she'd ruined her chances of bringing up her grade in the class.

19. Sophia struggled to keep her head above water she tried to yell but the water kept getting in her mouth.

20. The hurricane was devastating tall buildings crumbled and crashed to the ground.

21. It was a wonderful day at the park the children swam in the river collected rocks and insects and laughed all day the older kids played soccer the adults prepared the food supervised the children and played cards for a short while.

22. Caterpillars eat plants and can cause damage to some crops but adult butterflies feed primarily on flowers and do not cause any harm.

23. Both Jesse and I had many errands to do this morning Jesse had to go to the post office and the bookstore I had to go to the pharmacy the video store and the bank.

24. The butterfly is extraordinary it begins as an ugly caterpillar and turns into something colorful it almost looks like a piece of art.

# Subordinating conjunctions

**Subordinating conjunctions** connect dependent, or subordinate, clauses to independent clauses. An independent clause can stand alone as a complete sentence. A dependent clause requires an independent clause to be correct or even to make sense. Furthermore, a dependent clause always begins with a subordinate conjunction.

Following is a list of the most common subordinating conjunctions.

| | | | |
|---|---|---|---|
| after | because | if | unless |
| although | before | now that | until |
| as | even if | since | when |
| as if | even though | than | where |
| as though | except | though | while |

They will head home **after** they finish eating.
She enjoyed talking to him, **because** he was so smart.
Tom will not join the team **unless** he can be the captain.

Several subordinating conjunctions express time relationships: *after, before, until, when,* and *while.* These conjunctions indicate when the action of the dependent clause takes place in relation to the action of the independent clause.

He was a doctor **before** becoming a veterinarian.
Pedro waited in line **while** Vanessa looked for a place to sit.

The subordinating conjunction *because* introduces a clause that provides a reason for something. It answers the question "why."

She loves the Doors, **because** they sing catchy songs.

The subordinating conjunctions *(ever) since* and *now that* express one of two things: an explanation or a time relationship.

They cannot go to Mexico, **since** they do not have enough money.
We have been eager to watch the movie **ever since** we saw the preview.
**Now that** they have enough money, they are going to Mexico.

*Although, even though,* and *though* express exception or indicate that a condition exists despite some other condition.

She liked her old apartment, **although** it was small and smelly.
I was good at volleyball, **even though** I was short.
I hated his choice of music, **though** his voice was quite good.

When it follows a negative statement, the conjunction *unless* expresses requirements or conditions.

She can't be part of the band **unless** she sings well.

The dependent *if* clause expresses a condition that must be met, and the independent clause describes what will happen when that condition is met.

He can be part of the band *if* he plays guitar or drums.

> No punctuation is required before many subordinating conjunctions, especially those that express a time relationship, if the conjunction follows the independent clause.
>
> **Before** he became a professional surfer, he was a skater.
> He was a skater **before** he became a professional surfer.

The relative pronouns *who, whom, that, which,* and *whose* can also function like subordinating conjunctions, because they introduce dependent clauses.

The conjunction *than* may be used as a subordinating conjunction, often introducing an **elliptical clause**, that is, a clause in which information that is understood is omitted.

You speak English far better **than** I [do].
I like apple pie better **than** [I like] chocolate cake.

Colloquially, it is quite common to use *than* as a preposition.

Cathy is more talented **than** him.
My brother plays the piano better **than** me.

To be more precise, the verb in the dependent clause may be included, which requires *than* to be treated as a conjunction.

Cathy is more talented **than he is**.
My brother plays the piano better **than I do**.

EXERCISE
18·8

*Complete each sentence with the appropriate subordinating conjunction.*

1. I really liked my old apartment, _____ it was small and poorly lit.

2. You must buy a ticket _____ you can walk into the theater and watch a movie.

3. She will have to wait _____ the nurse calls her name to see the doctor.

4. He appreciates my mom's cooking skills, _____ she always makes good dishes.

5. They used to be friends _____ they had an argument.

6. Let's make a cake! You mix in the sugar _____ I beat the eggs.

7. They cannot cross the river, _____ they don't have a boat.

8. He was a great musician, _____ he was partly deaf.

9. The musician kept handing out his demo _____ he finally got signed by a music label.

10. She must be rich, _____ she wears a lot of expensive jewelry.

11. Everyone likes Sophia, _____ she is generous and friendly.

12. My father never answers his phone _____ I will try to call him.

13. Fortunately, the tennis tournament was over _____ the cold weather began.

14. You may have that puppy _____ you promise to take care of it.

15. Jason is older _____ she is by two weeks.

16. I'll finish cleaning the dishes _____ the news is over.

17. My dad was supportive of my academic choices _____ he had reservations.

18. The federal government will raise taxes _____ budget cuts can save enough money.

**EXERCISE**
**18·9**

*Combine each pair of sentences into one sentence using* until.

EXAMPLE    He can't use his computer. He hasn't bought a computer monitor yet.

*He can't use his computer until he buys a computer monitor.*

1. They can't leave. They have to feed the cats first.

   _____

2. Tell me the truth. I am not going to leave this room.

   _____

3. He can't pay his parking ticket. He hasn't received his paycheck.

   _____

4. Finally, Steve arrived. Before that, it had been a boring conversation.

   _____

5. When I go to bed at night, I like to read. After a while, I get sleepy.

   _____

**EXERCISE**
**18·10**

*Combine each pair of sentences into one sentence using* now that, *eliminating explanatory phrases if they are not necessary.*

EXAMPLE    We have to wear swimsuits. We had been shopping at the mall, but we're at the beach now.

*Now that we're at the beach, we have to wear swimsuits.*

1. Patrick used to share an apartment with a friend, but a couple of weeks ago he moved into a house. Now he can use his own furniture.

   _____

   _____

2. I've finally finished painting the kitchen. Now I can go running.

   _____

   _____

3. They have to wear warm clothes. It's winter now.

   _____

4. He just celebrated his 21st birthday. Now he can legally drink.

   _____

   _____

5. Charles used to ride his bike to school, but last month he bought a Jeep. Now he can drive to school.

   _____

   _____

6. The civil war has ended. A new government is being formed.

   _____

   _____

7. It's been a long, hard month, but the project is finally over. We can relax.

   _____

   _____

8. Do you want to go swimming? The water has gotten warmer.

   _____

   _____

9. My best friend got married this morning. He's a married man now, so he has more responsibilities.

   _____

   _____

10. I can get a job as a translator. I know English now.

    _____

# Adverbs that act as conjunctions

**Conjunctive adverbs** are also considered conjunctions, because they can be used to connect independent clauses. They also act as adverbs, because they modify one of the independent clauses.

Following is a list of the most commonly used conjunctive adverbs.

| | | | |
|---|---|---|---|
| afterwards | for example | nevertheless | therefore |
| anyway | for instance | next | thus |
| besides | however | now | unfortunately |
| consequently | instead | otherwise | |
| eventually | later | still | |
| finally | likewise | then | |

The car engine broke down; **consequently**, we did not finish the race.
I spent the day at the public library; **later**, I went for a walk to relax.
The thief lost his appeal; **therefore**, he was forced to go to prison.
She had a lot of bills this month; **unfortunately**, that means that she can't go on the trip with us.

**EXERCISE 18·11**

*Combine each pair of sentences into one sentence using a conjunctive adverb.*

EXAMPLE
The young man was single for years. He met the girl of his dreams.

*The young man was single for years; finally, he met the girl of his dreams.*

1. We stopped to visit our grandparents on our way to Oklahoma. We stayed with friends in Tulsa.

_____

_____

2. We had planned to go to the park today. The rain canceled our plans.

_____

_____

3. It was a difficult time for her. She learned a lot from the experience.

_____

_____

4. The hotel stayed vacant and abandoned for many years. The city council decided to tear it down.

_____

_____

5. They had a romantic walk along the river. They went back to the hotel to drink some champagne.

_____

_____

6. Mr. Williams cannot speak at the conference. Mr. Rogers will go in his place.

_____

_____

7. We enjoy all kinds of outdoor activities. We really like rock climbing.

_____

_____

8. The mall is already closed. You do not have any money to spend.

_____

_____

9. The essay must be written by Monday. You fall behind schedule.

_____

_____

10. Anna Nicole Smith was incredibly rich. She did not have a happy life.

_____

_____

11. They spent their entire afternoon shopping for clothes. They wore some of their purchases to the dance.

_____

_____

12. He likes seafood. He is allergic to oysters.

_____

_____

# Prepositions

**Prepositional phrases** are formed using a preposition and its object (a noun or a pronoun). Prepositional phrases describe the relationship between the object of the preposition and another element of a sentence. In general, prepositional phrases describe relationships of place, time, and ownership.

> The dog is hiding **under the car**.
> They only rented that apartment **for a month**.
> The back door **of my house** is painted blue.

Following is a list of commonly used prepositions.

| | | | | |
|---|---|---|---|---|
| about | before | despite | of | to |
| above | behind | down | off | toward |
| across | below | during | on | under |
| after | beneath | for | out | until |
| against | beside | from | over | up |
| along | besides | in | since | with |
| among | between | into | through | within |
| around | beyond | like | throughout | without |
| at | by | near | till | |

## Compound prepositions

A **compound preposition** functions as a single preposition, but is composed of more than one word. Just like other prepositions, a compound preposition is followed by a noun or pronoun object.

Following is a list of common compound prepositions.

| | | |
|---|---|---|
| ahead of | in addition to | in regard to |
| as far as | in back of | in spite of |
| because of | in case of | instead of |
| by means of | in lieu of | next to |
| contrary to | in light of | out of |

> They solved the problem **by means of** a special algorithm.
> **In case of** fire, do not use the elevators.
> **In spite of** his hard work, the promotion went to Jane Anderson.
> He ran **out of** the haunted house.

Whether simple or compound, prepositions function the same in sentences.

The preposition *between* expresses a choice involving two people or things, while the preposition *among* expresses a choice involving more than two people or things.

> She had to choose **between** going out or watching a movie at home.
> There is an enormous difference **between** love and hate.
> Just **between** you and me, I'd really like to go out with Juan's sister.

> The mood **among** the guests was quite festive.
> I have always counted you **among** my friends.
> **Among** the men in his squadron was a lad of only 19.

## EXERCISE 19·1

*In each sentence, underline the preposition(s), including compound prepositions, and their noun objects.*

1. He would prefer a hybrid car instead of the truck.

2. If they are still swimming in the pool, then they will be late for dinner.

3. The clouds floated high above the hills.

4. Tell me about the book you read.

5. George ran into the room and quickly took a seat next to Helen.

6. Is she the one you spoke of?

7. I recently got a letter from him while he was away in Iraq.

8. Contrary to public opinion, the election is not a foregone conclusion.

9. Sitting among the students was a professor from the philosophy department.

10. Are you satisfied with this table? I can get you another by the window.

## EXERCISE 19·2

*Complete each sentence with an appropriate object for each preposition.*

EXAMPLE    They had an argument with ___*their new neighbor*___.

1. She spent a lot of time alone in _____.

2. They had to borrow some furniture from _____.

3. I must choose between _____.

4. We cannot leave before _____, but we'll arrive there around

   _____.

5. Does she know the way to _____?

6. In spite of _____, they set out on the mountain hike.

7. In light of _____, I feel you should retake the course.

8. Among _____, he saw many old friends.

9. I've always been interested in _____.

10. Because of _____, the game had to be canceled.

# Noun and pronoun objects

The object of a prepositional phrase can be either a noun or a pronoun. In most cases, when a noun is replaced by a pronoun, the pronoun must be of the same number and gender as the noun.

> Ms. Harper spoke **of her son** quite often.
> Ms. Harper spoke **of him** quite often.
>
> He sat **on the old mare** and looked out over the valley.
> He sat **on her** and looked out over the valley.
>
> **In spite of the impending storm**, they set off for the park.
> **In spite of it**, they set off for the park.
>
> She never received the gift **from Tom and me**.
> She never received the gift **from us**.
>
> He danced **with the same two girls** all evening.
> He danced **with them** all evening.

However, if a prepositional phrase introduced by *in* indicates a location, a pronoun object sometimes cannot replace a noun object. Instead, it is more common to use an adverb, such as *here* or *there*. This is particularly true of cities and large regions.

> She loved living **in Washington, D.C.**
> She loved living **there**.
>
> We haven't been **in this town** for very long.
> We haven't been **here** for very long.

Compare the examples above with those below.

> The woman sat comfortably **in a comfy chair**.
> The woman sat comfortably **in it**.
>
> Richard found 50 dollars **in the little box**.
> Richard found 50 dollars **in it**.

Something similar occurs with the preposition *of* when it shows possession and, on occasion, with the preposition *by*. Although pronoun objects are quite acceptable following *of* and *by*, there is a tendency to use a possessive pronoun in place of the prepositional phrase.

> The color **of the blouse** is bright red.
> **Its** color is bright red.
>
> The roar **of the huge lion** gave me chills.
> **Its roar** gave me chills.

The quality **of his poems and short stories** was highly regarded.
**Their quality** was highly regarded.

The lecture **by Professor Helms** had an impact on us all.
**His lecture** had an impact on us all.

The raid on the house **by the police** was carried out in secret.
**Their raid** on the house was carried out in secret.

Although each of these sentences could have contained a prepositional phrase with a pronoun object, the tendency is to use a possessive pronoun instead of a prepositional phrase.

| | |
|---|---|
| POSSIBLE | The raid on the house by them was unwarranted. |
| MORE LIKELY | Their raid on the house was unwarranted. |

EXERCISE
19·3

*Rewrite each sentence, changing the prepositional phrase to one with a pronoun object or to an appropriate adverb.*

EXAMPLE    No students were allowed in the professors' lounge.
     *No students were allowed there.*

1. We spent a lot of time in Brooklyn.

   _____

2. They have been in Mexico for over three years.

   _____

3. In the drawer, I found my sister's diary.

   _____

4. City Hall has been located in this part of town for years.

   _____

5. What are you hiding in those little sacks?

   _____

*Now, rewrite each sentence, changing the prepositional phrase to the appropriate possessive pronoun.*

EXAMPLE    I met the brother of the governor of the state.
     *I met his brother.*

6. Do you really like the smell of cabbage soup?

   _____

7. The gowns of all three bridesmaids looked like flour sacks.

   _____

8.  A symphony by an old Viennese composer was recently found.

_____

9.  They said the poems of Emily Dickinson are their favorites.

_____

10. The political goals of America are slowly changing.

_____

# More than one prepositional phrase

Sentences are not limited to one prepositional phrase. Indeed, a series of prepositional phrases can occur in one sentence.

Look **in** the attic **in** a little box **on** the floor **behind** that old mattress.

Each prepositional phrase in this example gives further information about *where to look*.

| | |
|---|---|
| Where should I look? | in the attic |
| Where in the attic? | behind that old mattress |
| Where behind the mattress? | on the floor |
| Where on the floor? | in a little box |

Naturally, you cannot connect random prepositional phrases to form a sentence. They must make sense together and provide further information. Consider what might logically follow the prepositional phrases in these examples.

She spent the night in an old house . . .
She spent the night in an old house **located on a cliff near the Black River.**

The men worked on the roof . . .
The men worked on the roof **next to a chimney crumbling from years of neglect.**

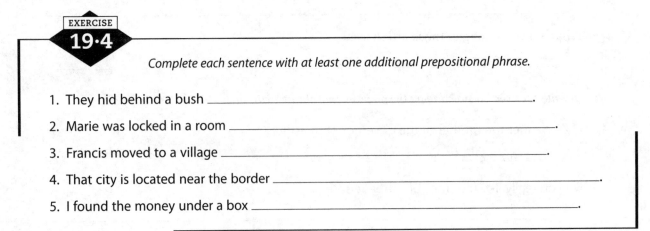

EXERCISE
19·4

*Complete each sentence with at least one additional prepositional phrase.*

1. They hid behind a bush _____.

2. Marie was locked in a room _____.

3. Francis moved to a village _____.

4. That city is located near the border _____.

5. I found the money under a box _____.

# Adjectives and adverbs

## Adjectives

**Adjectives** describe or modify a noun or pronoun. They provide more information about a noun or pronoun, and they can provide additional meaning for a noun phrase.

> Joseph is a **famous** guitar player.
> The **elderly** couple slept at last.

The list of English adjectives is, of course, quite long. Here are some frequently used examples.

| | | | |
|---|---|---|---|
| appropriate | generous | lonely | Spanish |
| beautiful | good | modern | spicy |
| bitter | intelligent | poor | tall |
| brown | lazy | rich | tasty |
| forgetful | local | scary | vintage |

An English adjective has only one form, whether the noun or pronoun it modifies is masculine, feminine, or neuter, or singular or plural. This is true for predicate adjectives, as well as for adjectives that stand before a noun.

> The new professor is quite **intelligent**.
> **Intelligent** people don't brag about their talents.

> His youngest son is terribly **lazy**.
> A **lazy** person probably won't go far in life.

> Even the baby giraffe is **tall**.
> That **tall** girl is the star of her basketball team.

## Adverbs

A primary function of **adverbs** is to modify verbs. Many adverbs are formed by adding the suffix *-ly* to adjectives: *quick ~ quickly, happy ~ happily, careful ~ carefully, bitter ~ bitterly.*

> She swims **quickly**.
> He opened the window **carefully**.

Adverbs can also modify adjectives, thereby augmenting their meaning.

> They are **extremely** sad.
> The crowd soon became **rather** unruly.

Several adverbs express time, for example, *tomorrow, today, never, soon, yesterday, yet.*

My parents are supposed to arrive **tomorrow**.
Will you be off the phone **soon**?
Has Jimmy taken his shower **yet**?

Some adverbs can be placed in the middle of a sentence, and they generally have a set position there. Mid-sentence adverbs stand in front of verbs in the simple present and simple past tenses. They follow forms of *be* in simple present and simple past tenses, and they stand between an auxiliary verb and a main verb.

BEFORE SIMPLE PRESENT AND PAST TENSES

We **seldom** have dessert after dinner.
My brother **often** spent his free time playing his guitar.
I **rarely** talk on the phone for more than a few minutes.
Tom **frequently** asks an embarrassing question.

FOLLOWING SIMPLE PRESENT AND PAST TENSES OF *be*

Anna is **always** there on time.
Bill was **sometimes** late for an appointment.
Her husband is **never** around when she needs him.
The children are **apparently** in very good health.

BETWEEN AN AUXILIARY VERB AND MAIN VERB

John can **never** face his parents again.
Anna has **always** gotten there on time.
They have **often** traveled abroad.
Do you **regularly** shop in this store?

EXERCISE
20·1

Rewrite each sentence, placing never *in the appropriate position. Then, rewrite the sentence with* rarely.

EXAMPLE    He spoke with his aunt.

_He never spoke with his aunt._

_He rarely spoke with his aunt._

1. We had arranged a surprise party for them.

   _____

   _____

2. The soprano from France sang at the Met.

   _____

   _____

3. Grandfather was in a good mood.

   _____

   _____

4. My brother could fix his own car.

_____

_____

5. They will go to Alaska in the winter.

_____

_____

The word *well* can be used as an adverb or as an adjective. As an adverb, *well* means "in a good manner" or "capably" and describes how someone does something. As an adjective, *well* means "healthy."

**EXERCISE**
**20·2**

*Underline the adjective(s) in each sentence.*

1. This book is hard to read.

2. This is the best article I have ever read.

3. She was beautiful and happy at her wedding.

4. If we are fast, we will find good seats for the movie.

5. The humid breezes blew across the plain.

6. They were beaming and radiant at their anniversary.

*Now, underline the adverb in each sentence.*

7. We hurriedly ran out of the burning building.

8. I rarely take any breaks in the morning.

9. Loudly, the teenagers moved through the school corridors.

10. She finally went to the grocery store after running out of toilet paper.

11. He often read the Bible in the morning.

12. The library receives a copy of the newspaper biweekly.

13. Our manager spoke to us seriously about behavioral issues.

14. The children ended by playing indoors.

15. Catherine regularly brings coffee to her co-workers.

16. I was still stuck in traffic.

17. Perhaps we will fly to Atlanta next month.

EXERCISE
20·3

*Underline the word that correctly completes each sentence.*

1. Joseph is a **meticulous** | **meticulously** writer. He writes **meticulous** | **meticulously**.

2. Catherine asked me an **easy** | **easily** question. I was unable to answer her question,

   but my friend Anjali answered it **easy** | **easily**.

3. Pedro speaks **loud** | **loudly**. He has a **loud** | **loudly** voice.

4. Because the movie had already started, I entered the movie theater **quiet** | **quietly**.

5. Sophie **secretive** | **secretly** liked the boy.

6. Ali speaks Arabic very **good** | **well**. He has very **good** | **well** pronunciation.

Some adverbs can modify not only verbs and adjectives, but other adverbs as well. The function of this small group of adverbs is to impart a quality or degree to the meaning of the adverb. A short list of these adverbs follows.

> a bit
> a little
> exceptionally
> extremely
> quite
> rather
> somewhat
> too
> very

Consider the difference in meaning in the following pairs of sentences.

> They were working fast.
> They were working **exceptionally** fast.
>
> The poor man wept bitterly.
> The poor man wept **quite** bitterly.
>
> She spoke rapidly.
> She spoke **too** rapidly.
>
> They approached the animal cautiously.
> They approached the animal **very** cautiously.

EXERCISE
20·4

*In each sentence, underline every adjective and adverb, marking each one* adj *(adjective)* or adv *(adverb).*

1. Sue opened the clean car door quite rapidly.

2. Moroccan jewelers carved beautiful pendants from ebony.

3. The old woman cooks the soup very carefully.

4. A busy person usually has rather short conversations on the phone.

5. The children had a very good time at the amusement park yesterday.

EXERCISE
20·5

*Rewrite each sentence, using the adverb in parentheses correctly in the sentence.*

1. Catherine has finished writing the essay due tomorrow. (already)

_____

2. Helen is at Jason's house. (seldom)

_____

3. Does he go to her house? (always)

_____

4. He goes hiking to get away from it all and relax. (often)

_____

5. She should tell him the truth. (always)

_____

6. Eric has seen the ocean. (never)

_____

7. Steven produces his electronic music on his laptop. (often)

_____

8. Anna is at the club on Tuesday nights. (often)

_____

9. Vince goes to the movies, because he prefers staying home. (rarely)

_____

10. I don't ask for a girl's number if I don't know her. (generally)

_____

11. I have eaten an Asian pear. (never)

_____

# Filler subjects and impersonal subjects

## Filler subjects

The word *there* can be used as a **filler subject**. It is commonly combined with forms of *be* together with the actual subject of the sentence. Although the word *there* is in the subject position of the sentence, it is actually the noun that follows the verb that is the subject and that determines whether the form of *be* is singular or plural.

> **There is** a dog sitting on my porch.
> **There are** 600 beds in this dormitory.
> **There were** four people injured in the attack.
> **There will be** a book waiting for you at the counter.

The word *there* is added to sentences like this to emphasize the existence of the subject of the sentence. It is possible to compose versions of such sentences without *there*.

> A dog is sitting on my porch.
> Six hundred beds are in this dormitory.
> Four people were injured in the attack.
> A book will be waiting for you at the counter.

Note that the noun subject uses an indefinite article when singular (*a/an*) and no article when plural or a collective.

> There is **a** dog sitting . . .    NOT  There is **the** dog sitting . . .
> There were four people . . .    NOT  There were **the** four people . . .
> There was frosting . . .    NOT  There was **the** frosting . . .

This expression can also be used with a variety of **auxiliaries**. In such cases, the verb *be* occurs as an infinitive or auxiliary.

> There **seems to be** a problem here.
> There **should be** more time spent solving this problem.
> There **has been** an accident on Route 10.
> There **have been** several robberies on this street.
> **Could** there **be** another reason for this problem?
> There **will** not **be** enough time for that.

This structure is also used when *be* is the auxiliary in a passive structure.

> There **were** two men **arrested** for the robbery.
> There **was** no one **blamed** for the accounting errors.

*There* can be used with a few other verbs, but sentences with such constructions often sound stilted or old-fashioned.

There **exists** a state of war between our two nations.
Soon there **developed** the question whether the craft would actually fly.

EXERCISE
21·1

*Rewrite each sentence, using* there *as the filler subject.*

1. A cat was sleeping under the coffee table.

   _____

2. Several girls were learning to dance ballet.

   _____

3. A class photo will be taken at ten sharp.

   _____

4. A lot of damage had been caused by the storm.

   _____

5. Promises are to be kept.

   _____

*Now, complete each sentence with an appropriate phrase.*

6. There was _____.

7. Has there been _____?

8. There will be _____.

9. There have been _____.

10. There are _____.

# Impersonal subjects

Besides being the personal pronoun that replaces a neuter singular noun, *it* is also used as the subject of the verb *be*, and occasionally of *become*. In such combinations, it forms an **impersonal subject**. The meaning of sentences with impersonal subjects gives the responsibility of the condition described in the sentence to *it*, a mysterious, unknown subject.

**It will be** sunny tomorrow.
**It is** very nice in Kingston, Jamaica.
**It was** too hot in that room.
**It will become** clear before too long.

When *it* is used as the personal pronoun replacement of a noun, its meaning is quite different. The impersonal subject, however, doesn't replace a noun. Compare the two uses of *it*.

PRONOUN REPLACEMENT

The house burned down. **It** burned down.
This essay by Einstein is hard to understand. **It** is hard to understand.
The struggle for peace never ends. **It** never ends.

IMPERSONAL SUBJECT

**It** was too late to go.
**It** became quite chilly.
Was **it** as humid last summer as **it** is this summer?

A subject repeated in consecutive sentences sounds awkward. This is true whether the subject is a noun, noun phrase, or pronoun.

The girls didn't dance. The girls didn't sing.
Speaking rudely to a professor is a mistake. Speaking rudely to a professor can get you in trouble.
It rained. It thundered. It poured for hours.

Conjunctions are used to combine such sentences and avoid repeated subjects.

The girls didn't dance **or** sing.
Speaking rudely to a professor is a mistake **and** can get you in trouble.
It rained, thundered, **and** poured for hours.

---

EXERCISE
21·2

*Complete each sentence with one of the following: an appropriate personal pronoun, there, or it.*

EXAMPLE My mom is a good leader. ___*She*___ is someone I look up to.

1. These youth summer camps really had an impact on my teenage years.

   _____ helped to make me who I am today.

2. Volunteers work very hard, and humanitarian organizations appreciate them very much.

   Usually, _____ become very close to the people _____ work with.

3. Yesterday, _____ rained for over five hours.

4. In Switzerland, _____ is essential to speak French to get a job that pays well.

5. At the county jail, _____ are a lot of teacher volunteers who can help inmates prepare for exams.

6. My teacher tries to help us understand. For example, in math class _____ often spends a long time on complicated equations.

7. I come from Spain. There _____ take three-hour lunch breaks.

8. Stress is awful. Actually, _____ is one of the most negative feelings someone could have.

9. I see you have a new car. When did you buy _____?

10. I believe _____ was in 1929 when _____ happened.

*Fill in the blanks with* it *or* there.

My cabin is in the back of the boat. It is a small cabin, but it is very cozy.

In addition to a single bunk bed and a minuscule dresser, _____ is a small

desk in the corner of the cabin. On the bed _____ is a plaid bedspread.

When _____ is raining, _____ is prohibited to open the window.

When _____ is sunny, I can look out the window and see the ocean for miles

and miles. _____ isn't much room for anything in the cabin, but I don't mind it.

While the cabin is very little, to me _____ seems perfect.

*Decide if the italicized word* it *in each sentence is a personal pronoun (PP) or
an impersonal pronoun (IP), then write PP or IP in the blank.*

EXAMPLE    When *it* started to rain, we ran for the shelter. ___IP___

1. He bought an old camera in Seattle. He found *it* in an antique shop downtown. _____

2. We stayed in a motel that night. When we got up the next day, *it* had begun to snow.

   _____

3. This article on chemistry was good. *It* was rather easy reading. _____

4. The streets are so confusing. *It* was rather easy to get lost. _____

5. *It* sleeted all night long. _____ *It* wasn't until morning that we saw how slick the streets

   had become. _____

# ·22· Clauses

A group of words that has a subject and a verb is called a **clause**. A clause may or may not be a complete sentence. There are two kinds of clauses: independent clauses and dependent clauses.

## Independent clauses

An **independent clause**, or main clause, is a complete sentence. It contains the main subject and verb of the sentence.

> Alex goes to work.
> The children are doing their homework.
> It turned quite cold.

In addition to the subject and verb of a clause, other elements may be added to the beginning, middle, or end of the clause to provide more information. These elements can be adverbs, prepositional phrases, or even other clauses.

| | |
|---|---|
| ADVERB | Alex **rarely** goes to work. |
| PREPOSITIONAL PHRASE | **In the summer**, Alex goes to work on his bike. |
| RELATIVE CLAUSE | Alex, **who is my husband's best friend**, goes to work with me. |

## Dependent clauses

A **dependent clause** cannot stand on its own and make complete sense. It must be connected to an independent clause. Consider the following examples, which sound strange when they stand alone; they are dependent on another clause to complete their meaning.

> Although he likes it a lot.
> When we visited Portugal.
> Since he arrived here last June.
> While the baby was still asleep.

These clauses have a subject and a verb, but they do not express a complete idea. A dependent clause, by itself, is called a **sentence fragment**.

You can often recognize a dependent clause by the presence of a **subordinating conjunction**. "*Because* he is on time" is a dependent clause, whereas "He is on time" is an independent clause.

124

The following sentences combine the dependent clauses in the examples above with independent clauses to make complete sentences.

> Although he likes it a lot, he won't spend that much for the car.
> When we visited Portugal, we came upon a beautiful mountain village.
> Since he arrived here last June, he has refused to go out and find a job.
> John and Mary cleaned up the family room while the baby was still asleep.

Following is a list of the most common conjunctions that could begin a dependent clause.

| | | | |
|---|---|---|---|
| after | because | since | when |
| although | before | so | whenever |
| as | even though | though | whether |
| as long as | if | unless | while |
| as soon as | in order that | until | |

The relative pronouns *who, which,* and *that* also introduce a dependent clause.

**EXERCISE**
**22·1**

*Underline the independent clause in each sentence.*

1. If Mary gets here early, she will be able to eat some dessert.

2. Before he went to his class, Marco picked up something from the office.

3. William read the cover story of *The Economist* while he waited for lunchtime.

4. Barbara laughed when she heard the joke.

5. Paul watched as the woman slapped the teenager who had insulted her.

6. Even though alcohol is bad for your liver, many people enjoy drinking a lot of it.

# Relative clauses

A **relative clause** is a dependent clause that modifies an antecedent noun or pronoun in an independent clause. It identifies, describes, or otherwise provides information about the antecedent.

The subject pronouns for a relative clause are *who, which,* and *that.* In the following examples, note how two independent sentences are connected by a relative pronoun to make one single complete sentence.

> I thanked my dad. **My dad** brought me my house keys.
> I thanked my dad, **who** brought me my house keys.
>
> They live in Seattle. **Seattle** is on the Pacific Ocean.
> They live in Seattle, **which** is on the Pacific Ocean.
>
> She has the information. **The information** will clear my name.
> She has the information **that** will clear my name.

If the same noun or pronoun occurs in two sentences as illustrated above, the second clause can be changed to a relative clause by combining the two clauses with a relative pronoun. The repeated noun or pronoun in the second clause is changed to a relative pronoun.

Note that the subject or object of two such clauses can be considered identical even if one is the pronoun replacement of the other.

> The laptop is mine. **It** is on the table.
> The laptop **that** is on the table is mine.
>
> I spoke with her mother. **She** said that Laura was out of town.
> I spoke with her mother, **who** said that Laura was out of town.

*Who* is used for people, *which* is used for things, and *that* is used for both people and things. But there is another difference to be considered between *who, which,* and *that. Who* and *which* introduce relative clauses that are **parenthetical** in nature—they provide nonessential information about the antecedent.

> The governor, **who** is visiting Canada right now, was elected in a landslide.
> This orchard, **which** was planted by my grandfather, produces 1,000 bushels of apples
>     each year.

The relative pronoun *that* introduces a clause that provides *essential* information about its antecedent.

> The governor **that** was recently elected received a standing ovation.
> The orchard **that** was destroyed by insects was planted by my grandfather.

**Commas** separate a clause introduced by *who* or *which,* but not a clause introduced by *that.*

If the relative pronoun is an object in the relative clause, *who* is changed to *whom* in formal speech and writing; *whom* is not often used in casual speech. When the relative pronoun *that* is the object of its clause, it can be omitted.

> The men **that** they rewarded for their bravery are out of work.
> The men they rewarded for their bravery are out of work.
>
> The watch **that** he found on the sidewalk is priceless.
> The watch he found on the sidewalk is priceless.

Prepositions, which require the object form of *who* and *which,* can stand in more than one position in a relative clause: at the beginning or the end.

> The men **about whom** she plans to write an article are out of work.
> The men **that** she plans to write an article **about** are out of work.
>
> The article **from which** we got the information is about global warming.
> The article **that** we got the information **from** is about global warming.

If the relative pronoun is *that,* the position of the preposition is always at the end of the clause and *that* can be omitted.

> The books **that** you asked **for** are on your desk.
> The books you asked **for** are on your desk.

*Combine each pair of sentences into one, using the second sentence as a relative clause.*

1. The student is from Korea. She sits next to me.

   _____

2. The boy is excited. He won first prize.

   _____

3. I smelled the cake. It was cooling on the window ledge.

   _____

4. We are studying English. It involves learning many rules.

   _____

5. We are studying sentences. They contain different clauses.

   _____

6. I am using a relative clause. It includes a possessive pronoun.

   _____

7. Physics problems require long calculations. They are often very complex.

   _____

8. The bus driver was friendly. He spoke to me a lot.

   _____

9. I liked that girl. I met her at the zoo last week.

   _____

10. The movie was awful. I saw it.

    _____

11. I liked the poem. He wrote it.

    _____

12. His grandparents were very nice. We visited them last month.

    _____

Combine each pair of sentences into one, using the second sentence of each exercise as a relative clause in two different ways.

EXAMPLE    The child was loud. I heard him late last night.

_The child, whom I heard late last night, was loud._

_The child I heard late last night was loud._

1. I must thank your brother. I received flowers from him.

_____

_____

2. The woman was very kind. I spoke with her this morning.

_____

_____

3. The conference was interesting. I registered for it.

_____

_____

4. The painting was colorful and detailed. I was looking at it for a long time.

_____

_____

5. The man is sleeping over there. I was telling you about him.

_____

_____

## Indefinite relative pronouns

Compound forms of the relative pronoun—*whoever, whomever, whatever,* and *whichever*—are called **indefinite relative pronouns**, because they do not refer to a specific person or thing.

> **Whoever** finishes first wins a prize. (*one of the contestants*)
> The manager selects **whomever** she wants for the job. (*one of the employees*)
> The man just blurted out **whatever** came to mind. (*one of his thoughts*)
> Pick **whichever** of the two books interests you. (*one of the books*)

*Who* and *what* can also be used as an indefinite relative pronouns. They replace the old-fashioned and awkward phrases *him who* and *that which.*

> I don't know **him who** arrived. ~ I don't know **who** arrived.
> I'll tell you **that which** is important. ~ I'll tell you **what** is important.

Indefinite *who* and *what* can also be used as objects in a relative clause.

Mr. Cole asked **about whom** the letter was written.
They announced **who** the new chancellor will be.

She didn't understand **what** you were talking **about**.
Do you have any idea **what** the woman wanted?

## Possessive relative pronouns

*Whose* is used to indicate possession. Like other possessive pronouns (*my, your, his, her, its, our, their*), it is used to modify a noun. The possessive pronoun and the noun are placed at the beginning of the relative clause.

I know this lady. **Her purse** was stolen.
I know this lady **whose purse** was stolen.

The man paints well. I saw **his exposition**.
The man, **whose exposition** I saw, paints well.

*Whose* may also replace a possessive noun.

They located the woman. **The woman's mother** had become ill.
They located the woman **whose mother** had become ill.

Can you help the tourists? **The tourists' visas** have expired.
Can you help the tourists **whose visas** have expired?

EXERCISE
22·4

*Combine each pair of sentences into one, using the second sentence as a relative clause.*

EXAMPLE     My neighbor is very nice. I am walking her dog.
  *My neighbor, whose dog I am walking, is very nice.*

1. Mr. Castro teaches a class for foreign students. His native language is Spanish.

   _____

2. The yoga instructor is excellent. I am taking his class.

   _____

3. I met the man. His son is my office manager.

   _____

4. The woman called 911. The woman's apartment was on fire.

   _____

5. I laughed at the man. I pushed him in the pool.

   _____

6. I come from France. Its history goes back hundreds of years.

   _____

7. The people were crazy. We visited their house.

_____

8. I sleep in a hotel. Its residents are very noisy.

_____

9. I have to call the girl. I accidentally picked up her cell phone after our date.

_____

10. The boy put lotion all over his face. His cheeks got sunburned while he was lying at the swimming pool.

_____

_____

EXERCISE
22·5

Underline the relative clause in each sentence.

EXAMPLE   The car _that he is driving_ is brand new.

1. The fireman who put out the fire was very fast.

2. The friends I was waiting for were late.

3. The shoes that she is wearing are handmade.

4. The project Peter is working on must be finished by March.

5. The person whose advice I take most seriously is my mom.

6. Did I tell you about the accident I had last week?

7. The man I was talking to pushed me out of the way.

8. Did you hear about the explosion that destroyed the embassy?

EXERCISE
22·6

Combine each pair of sentences into one, using the second sentence as a relative clause in two different ways, where possible. Some pairs of sentences permit only one wording of the relative clause.

EXAMPLE   The child was loud. I heard him late last night.

_The child, whom I heard late last night, was loud._

_The child I heard late last night was loud._

1. The younger men are from Peru. We met them in the hotel lobby this morning.

   _____

   _____

2. I explained my absence to the manager. I had missed his presentation.

   _____

   _____

3. Yesterday, I ran into Paul. I hadn't seen him in months.

   _____

4. The driver missed the red light. He was not paying attention.

   _____

5. He spoke of the postmodern movement. I know nothing about it.

   _____

   _____

6. The historian is well known for his research. We met him in Paris.

   _____

   _____

7. I am reading a novel. It was written by Alexander Dumas.

   _____

8. The teacher gave good explanations. I questioned him.

   _____

   _____

9. The professor gives easy exams. I passed his class.

   _____

10. I returned the car. I had borrowed it from my father.

    _____

    _____

11. The hunter caught the lion. It had killed someone from the village.

    _____

    _____

12. The children are very quiet. I am taking care of them.

    _____

    _____

# Where

In a relative clause, *where* refers to a place in the independent clause and replaces a prepositional phrase indicating location. The preposition from the phrase replaced by *where* is not used.

> The house is new. He lives **in the house**.
> The house **where** he lives is new.
> The house, **in which** he lives, is new.
> The house, **which** he lives **in**, is new.
> The house **that** he lives **in** is new.
> The house he lives **in** is new.

> The barn caught fire. They were playing **inside the barn**.
> The barn, **where** they were playing, caught fire.
> The barn, **inside which** they were playing, caught fire.
> The barn, **which** they were playing **inside**, caught fire.
> The barn **that** they were playing **inside** caught fire.
> The barn they were playing **inside** caught fire.

*Where* may also replace *there* in such clauses.

> The house is new. He lives **there**.
> The house **where** he lives is new.

### EXERCISE
### 22·7

*Combine each pair of sentences into one, using the second sentence as a relative clause.*

1. That is the cafeteria. I will eat lunch in the cafeteria.

   _____

2. The medieval village was beautiful. We spent our summer there.

   _____

3. The neighborhood is dangerous. I grew up in the neighborhood.

   _____

4. That is the account. I kept all my savings in the account.

   _____

5. Carl is from Jamaica. I used to live there.

   _____

# When

In a relative clause, *when* refers to a time expression in the independent clause and replaces an adverbial expression of time. The preposition accompanying a noun (*on that day, in that year, at that time, in that century,* and so on) is used before *which*. Otherwise, the preposition is omitted. *When* may also replace *then* in such clauses.

> I'll never forget that day. I cried a lot **that day**.  (I cried a lot **then**.)
> I'll never forget that day, **when** I cried a lot.

I'll never forget that day, **on which** I cried a lot.
I'll never forget that day **that** I cried a lot.
I'll never forget that day I cried a lot.

Time expressions use various prepositions, but *when* replaces the entire prepositional phrase, including the preposition.

She came in May. The weather is better then.
She came in May, **when** the weather is better.

It happened on Monday. He was still at home then.
It happened on Monday, **when** he was still at home.

I'll be there next week. Exams will be finished next week.
I'll be there next week, **when** exams will be finished.

Everyone left the party. The band stopped playing after the party.
Everyone left the party **when** the band stopped playing.

EXERCISE
22·8

*Combine each pair of sentences into one, using the second sentence as a relative clause with* when.

1. 1:10 pm is the time. My train arrives at the station then.

_____

2. June is the month. I will come in June.

_____

3. 1959 is the year. The Cuban socialist revolution took place then.

_____

4. Wednesday is the day. My plane arrives on Wednesday.

_____

EXERCISE
22·9

*Rewrite each sentence, using* where *in a relative clause. Begin your response with* That + *a form of* be.

EXAMPLE      She often shops in that store.
             *That is the store where she often shops.*

1. I was parked on that sidewalk.

_____

2. I was born in that city.

_____

3. You do your grocery shopping at that store.

_____

4. You keep your money at that bank.

_____

5. He works in that building.

_____

6. She lives on that street.

_____

7. We ate lunch at that Mexican restaurant.

_____

8. We have class in that amphitheater.

_____

9. We spent our vacation in that hotel.

_____

10. You went fishing in that river.

_____

11. I lived in that town until I was ten years old.

_____

12. Your father went to graduate school at that university.

_____

**EXERCISE**

**22·10**

*Answer each question according to the example. Do not use a relative pronoun.*

EXAMPLE    You played the record. Was it good?  (no)
           *No, the record I played was not good.*

1. You watched a movie. Was it scary?  (yes)

_____

2. You drank some iced coffee. Did it taste good?  (no)

_____

3. You bought a scarf. Does it keep your neck warm?  (yes)

_____

4. You had Chinese noodles for dinner. Were they too spicy? (no)

_____

5. You talked to a man. Did he answer your questions? (yes)

_____

6. You saw a little girl. Was she wearing a pink sweater? (no)

_____

7. You went to the football game. Was it exciting? (yes)

_____

8. You stayed at a bed-and-breakfast. Was it in the countryside? (no)

_____

9. You are finishing an exercise. Is it difficult? (no)

_____

10. You got a letter in the mail. Was it from your aunt? (no)

_____

EXERCISE
**22·11**

*Combine each pair of sentences into one, using a relative clause with* whose.

1. Neil Young is a musician. You are listening to his album.

_____

2. Aline Helg is a professor. I am writing a thesis for her class.

_____

3. Mr. Mohammed is a student. I found his notes.

_____

4. Paul is an intern. I borrowed his pen.

_____

5. The child began to scream. You lost his ball.

_____

6. Your neighbors are very funny. You stayed at your neighbor's house.

_____

7. An executive has been in a meeting for five hours. The executive's office is locked.

_____

8. A woman's necklace was stolen. The woman called a private detective.

   _____

9. Basquiat is an artist. You like his paintings the best.

   _____

10. Everyone tried to help the mother. Her car had broken down.

   _____

## Relative clauses that modify pronouns

Relative clauses can modify indefinite pronouns; the relative pronoun is usually omitted when it is the object of the clause.

> **Anybody who** wants to come is welcome.  (SUBJECT)
> There is **someone** I want to talk to.  (OBJECT)
> **Everything** he paints is ugly.  (OBJECT)

Other indefinite pronouns that follow this pattern are *anything, everyone, no one,* and *nothing.*
   Relative clauses can also modify *the one(s)* and *those.* The relative pronoun is used when it is the subject of the clause.

> Financial aid is available for **those who** really need it.  (SUBJECT)
> Jeffrey was **the only one** I knew at the meeting.  (OBJECT)

EXERCISE
22·12

*Complete each sentence with a relative clause.*

EXAMPLE     Scream at Tammy. She is the only one ___*who is to blame for the accident*___.

1. Peter makes a good first impression. He charms everyone _____.

2. I know someone _____.

3. Ask Margaret. She's the only one _____.

4. I'm powerless to help her. There's nothing _____.

5. We can't trust anyone. There's no one _____.

6. You can believe him. Everything _____.

7. All of the guests are seated. The host is the only one _____.

8. The test we took today was more difficult than the one _____.

9. The show has already begun. Those _____ had to wait until the end of the first scene to be seated.

10. The group was divided in half. Those _____ were told to go left.

    Those _____ were asked to take the right tunnel.

# Expressing quantity in relative clauses

Quantity can be expressed in a relative clause with the preposition *of* following an expression of quantity, such as *most, many,* or *some.* The relative pronoun (*whom, which,* or *whose*) follows *of.*

In my office, there are 12 people. **Most of them** are graduate students.
In my office, there are 12 people, **most of whom** are graduate students.

She gave us several tips. **Only a few of them** were useful.
She gave us several tips, **only a few of which** were useful.

The team captains discussed John. **One of his** problems was lack of discipline.
The team captains discussed John, **one of whose** problems was lack of discipline.

Following are some commonly used expressions that can introduce quantity in a relative clause.

| | | | |
|---|---|---|---|
| all of | (a) few of | most of | a number of |
| both of | (a) little of | neither of | some of |
| each of | many of | none of | two of |

EXERCISE
22·13

*Combine each pair of sentences into one, using the second sentence as a relative clause.*

EXAMPLE    He found several books. One of the books was in French.

_He found several books, one of which was in French._

1. Last night, the Metropolitan Movie Theater showed three of Stanley Kubrick's movies. One of them was *Dr. Strangelove.*

   _____

   _____

2. The village has three schools. Two of them are high schools.

   _____

3. I tried on three hats. I liked one of them.

   _____

4. The capital has about five million people. The majority of them are poor.

   _____

   _____

5. The army currently employs thousands of young men. All of them have obtained their GED.

   _____

   _____

6. After the riots in Paris, over 400 people were arrested. Many of them were peaceful protesters.

   _____

   _____

7. They spread rumors about Catherine. One of her faults was being beautiful beyond belief.

_____

_____

_____

EXERCISE

22·14

*Complete the relative clause in each sentence with words of your choice.*

1. The Turners own four dogs, one of _____.

2. Sylvia introduced me to her best friends, one of _____.

3. I have three aunts, all of _____.

4. I am taking three flights, one of _____.

5. I have two sisters, neither of _____.

6. The company hired four new secretaries, one of _____.

7. Last year I read about 20 books, four of _____.

8. In my parents' house, there are six guest rooms, several of _____

_____.

# Noun + *of which*

A relative clause may begin with a noun followed by *of which*. This construction, which is primarily used in formal written English, is a form of the possessive.

> He has an antique Japanese table. **The top of it** is made from ebony.
> He has an antique Japanese table, **the top of which** is made from ebony.

In less formal style, the sentence would be as follows.

> He has an antique Japanese table, **whose top** is made from ebony.

EXERCISE

22·15

*Combine each pair of sentences into one, using the second sentence as a relative clause with the formal* of which.

1. They bought an original Matisse painting. The value of the painting cannot possibly be estimated.

_____

_____

2. I bought a newspaper. The name of the newspaper is *Le Monde.*

_____

3. We visited a Victorian castle. The interior of the castle was made of wood.

_____

4. The United Nations is going through many changes. The outcome of these changes might alter human history.

_____

_____

5. My store's income is dependent on souvenirs. The sale of the souvenirs depends on the number of tourists.

_____

_____

## *Which* as the relative pronoun for an entire clause

An entire clause can be referred to by the relative pronoun *which*. This occurs when the relative pronoun refers not to one element in the main clause, but to the entire concept described in that clause.

> Robin was early. **That** surprised everyone.
> Robin was early, **which** surprised everyone.

In this example, no one was surprised by *Robin*. No one was surprised by the *early (time)*. But everyone was surprised by the entire idea that *Robin was early*. The antecedent of *which* is, therefore, the entire main clause.

> The escalator is out of order. **This** is rather inconveniencing.
> The escalator is out of order, **which** is rather inconveniencing.
>
> Both Tom and Laura won prizes. **That** made Dad very proud.
> Both Tom and Laura won prizes, **which** made Dad very proud.
>
> Marco falls asleep in class every day. **This** is unacceptable.
> Marco falls asleep in class every day, **which** is unacceptable.

EXERCISE
22·16

*Combine each pair of sentences into one, using the second sentence as a relative clause, the antecedent of which is the entire main clause.*

1. Clara was expelled from school. That took her family by surprise.

_____

2. My husband never washes the dishes. This annoys me.

_____

3. Pedro isn't home yet. That concerns me.

_____

4. There was a fire in Key West. This means many villas burned.

_____

5. I shut the car door on my finger. That was really silly of me.

_____

*Write an appropriate sentence on the first line, then combine the pair of sentences into one, using a relative clause.*

EXAMPLE    *My pants came off when I jumped in the pool*. That embarrassed me.
           *My pants came off when I jumped in the pool, which embarrassed me.*

1. _____. That distracted me a lot.

_____

2. _____. That shocked us all.

_____

3. _____. That means she'll be
home anytime.

_____

4. _____. I enjoyed that very much.

_____

5. _____. That was unexpected
good news.

_____

6. _____. That bothered me.

_____

7. _____. That annoyed me so
much that I could not fall asleep.

_____

8. _____. That was so loud that
it gave me a headache.

_____

# Noun clauses

A **noun clause** can be used as a subject or an object. It is composed of a noun and other elements that are used as a single entity—the subject or object of the sentence.

SUBJECT

**What he brought** was beautiful.
**What he brought back** was beautiful.
**What he brought back in his suitcase** was beautiful.

OBJECT

I saw **what he photographed**.
I saw **what he photographed with an old camera**.
I saw **what he skillfully photographed with an old camera**.

Following is a list of words that can introduce noun clauses.

| | | |
|---|---|---|
| how | when | who |
| if | where | whom |
| that | whether | whose |
| what | which | why |

## Noun clauses that begin with a question word

Noun clauses can be used as part of a response to a question.

| | |
|---|---|
| QUESTION | Where do they study? |
| RESPONSE | I don't know **where** they study. |
| QUESTION | Who built this castle? |
| RESPONSE | No one has any idea **who** built this castle. |

When used as a noun clause, the original question becomes either the subject or the object of the new sentence.

| | |
|---|---|
| SUBJECT | **What she thought about Bill** was best kept a secret. |
| OBJECT | I have no idea **what she thought about Bill**. |

Whereas *do, does,* and *did* are used to form questions with many verbs, they are never used in a noun clause.

| | |
|---|---|
| QUESTION | What **did** she **buy** at the store? |
| RESPONSE | I don't know what she **bought** at the store. |
| QUESTION | What time **does** Tom's plane **arrive**? |
| RESPONSE | Mom knows what time Tom's plane **arrives**. |

Note that the subject of a noun clause always precedes the verb, whether the question word is the subject or not. The question word is always the first element of a noun clause.

Who is in the backyard? (SUBJECT = who)
I wonder **who is in the backyard**.

What is she doing? (SUBJECT = she)
**What she is doing** is terribly wrong.

Where are the boys now? (SUBJECT = boys)
No one knows **where the boys are now**.

On what day will they arrive? (SUBJECT = they)
I know **on what day they will arrive**.

*Rewrite the question in parentheses, changing it to a noun clause in the new sentence.*

EXAMPLE    (What were they excited about?) <u>*What they were excited about*</u> was to be kept a secret.

1. (What was she mad about?) _____. was important.

2. (How well read is she?) I don't know _____.

3. (Where do you go shoe shopping?) Please tell me _____

    _____.

4. (How old is that child?) I have no idea _____.

5. (Whose pencil is this?) Do you know _____?

6. (Who are those men?) I don't know _____.

7. (Who is coming to the meeting?) I can't tell _____.

8. (Which flavor of ice cream does she want?) Let's ask her _____

    _____.

9. (How expensive is it?) I can't recall _____.

10. (What did he send you?) I forgot _____.

11. (What did she say to you?) _____ is a lie!

12. (Why did you leave the state?) _____ is a mystery.

13. (What are we doing at work?) _____ is top secret.

14. (What are we doing in English class today?) _____

    _____ is easy.

15. (Whom is she dating?) _____ is none of your business.

16. (Who is the president of Enron?) I don't know _____

    _____.

17. (How old does someone have to be in order to drink?) I need to look up

    _____.

*Rewrite each sentence as a question based on the information in italics.*

EXAMPLE    That girl is *from West Africa*.

_____Where is that girl from?_____

1. George was late for registration, *because he slept in*.

_____

2. It is *two hours* from San Antonio to the Mexican border.

_____

3. Sarah sold *a blue painting*.

_____

4. Pedro resides *in Chicago*.

_____

5. That woman is *Rita Davis*.

_____

6. That is *Jamie's* computer.

_____

7. Joseph saw *Peter* at the dinner.

_____

8. Sophie likes *this* movie best, *not that other one*.

_____

9. *Vicente* noticed Barbara at the bar.

_____

10. The train is scheduled to arrive *at noon*.

_____

*Change each question you created in Exercise 22-19 into a noun clause, using the blanks provided.*

EXAMPLE    (Where is that girl from?) I want to know ___*where that girl is from*___.

1. The administrative assistant wants to know _____.

2. He needs to know _____.

3. I don't know _____.

4. I want to know _____.

5. I want to know _____.

6. Jessica wants to know _____.

7. I ignored _____.

8. I don't know _____.

9. I want to know _____.

10. Could you please tell me _____?

## Noun clauses that begin with *whether* or *if*

*Whether* or *if* is used to introduce a clause when a **yes/no question** is changed to a noun clause. *If* often replaces *whether* in casual speech.

> Will they come?
> I don't know **whether they will come.**
> I don't know **if they will come.**
>
> Does she need assistance?
> I wonder **whether she needs assistance.**
> I wonder **if she needs assistance.**

The phrase *or not* is sometimes included in the noun clause.

> I wonder **whether or not** they will come.
> I wonder **whether** they will come **or not.**
> I wonder **if** she will come **or not.**

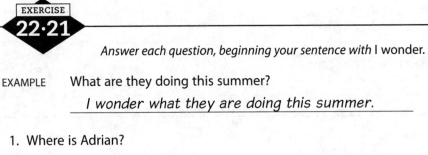

EXERCISE
22·21

*Answer each question, beginning your sentence with* I wonder.

EXAMPLE  What are they doing this summer?

*I wonder what they are doing this summer.*

1. Where is Adrian?

_____

2. Who took the television remote?

_____

3. Should you call her?

_____

4. Does Marie need any help?

_____

5. Did you leave your keys on the counter?

_____

6. Who is that man?

_____

7. What are they doing?

_____

8. Is she in trouble?

_____

9. Should we offer to help him?

_____

10. Do we have enough time to go on vacation?

_____

11. Whose bike is this?

_____

12. Why is the grass so green?

_____

13. How long does a bonsai live?

_____

14. Is there life on Mars?

_____

15. How was the earth created?

_____

## Noun clauses that begin with *that*

*That* can introduce a noun clause. It has no meaning per se, which is why it is often omitted, particularly in spoken English.

> She is a good cook.
> We all think **that** she is a good cook.
> We all think she is a good cook.
>
> The sea is blue.
> I know **that** the sea is blue.
> I know the sea is blue.

However, *that* cannot be omitted if the noun clause is used as the subject of the sentence.

> She doesn't like silent movies.
> **That** she doesn't like silent movies comes as a surprise to me.

The pronoun *it* often introduces a main clause that is followed by a noun clause introduced by *that*.

It comes as a surprise to me **that** she doesn't like silent movies.
It is well known **that** there is corruption at City Hall.

**EXERCISE**
**22·22**

*Change each sentence into a noun clause, first using* It is *plus the expression in parentheses, and then using* that *to introduce the noun clause.*

EXAMPLE     The ice is cold.  (a fact)

_It is a fact that the ice is cold._

_That the ice is cold is a fact._

1. Some immigrants don't receive equal pay for equal work.  (unfair)

_____

_____

2. Patricia has not been able to make it to second grade.  (too bad)

_____

_____

3. Alcohol abuse can ruin one's life.  (a well-known fact)

_____

_____

4. The sun is a star.  (a fact)

_____

_____

5. Smoking can cause lung cancer.  (true)

_____

_____

6. Marc has made no friends here.  (strange)

_____

_____

7. English is the principal language of the international business community.  (obvious)

_____

_____

# Question words and infinitives

Question words and *whether* may be followed by infinitives. The infinitive replaces the subject of the clause plus *should, can,* or *could.*

Peter can't decide **whether he should go** or **stay** at the office.
Peter can't decide **whether to go** or **(to) stay** at the office.

I don't know **whether I should laugh** or **cry.**
I don't know **whether to laugh** or **(to) cry.**

Please tell her **how she can get** to the nearest post office.
Please tell her **how to get** to the nearest post office.

Alicia told me **where I could** buy a cheap scooter.
Alicia told me **where to buy** a cheap scooter.

**EXERCISE 22·23**

*Complete each sentence with an appropriate infinitive or infinitive phrase.*

1. I was confused, and I wasn't sure what _____.

2. She's got so many dresses. She can't decide which _____
to the party.

3. I would like to live on the East Side, but I also like downtown. I can't decide whether

_____.

4. I can't wait to begin soccer practice. Do you know how _____

_____?

5. I have been looking around all day, and I don't know what _____

_____ for their anniversary.

6. Before you go to Marfa, go visit their Web site. It tells you where _____

and when _____.

7. My mom is hesitant. She doesn't know whether _____ or

_____.

**EXERCISE 22·24**

*Rewrite each sentence, replacing the subject and auxiliary verb in the noun clause with an infinitive.*

EXAMPLE     They told me whom I should look for.

They told me ___*whom to look for*___.

1. Please let me know where I can meet up with you.

_____

2. The fireman told me how I could stop a fire from spreading.

_____

_____

3. She told me when I should get there.

_____

4. Elizabeth liked two puppies, but she had trouble deciding which one she should take home.

_____

_____

5. Alex played in a rock band that was successful, but Nathalie didn't know whether she should buy their new album or not.

_____

_____

# The subjunctive

After certain main verbs, a noun clause beginning with *that* requires its verb to be subjunctive. The subjunctive form of a verb is its base form, for example, *run, be,* and *show.*

> The law demands that we **be** fair.
> I insisted that she **stop** by my house.
> I suggested that he not **go** to the football game.
> It is important that she **be** told where to sit.

Following is a list of common verbs and expressions that require a subjunctive verb in a noun clause introduced by *that.*

| | | |
|---|---|---|
| advise (that) | it is essential (that) | recommend (that) |
| ask (that) | it is important (that) | request (that) |
| demand (that) | it is necessary (that) | suggest (that) |
| insist (that) | it is vital (that) | |
| it is crucial (that) | propose (that) | |

### EXERCISE
### 22·25

*Complete each sentence with an appropriate verb phrase in the subjunctive.*

EXAMPLE    I suggest you tell him everything you __*know*__ .

1. I must insist that the man _____.

2. The judge recommends that we _____.

3. The lawyer demanded that she _____.

4. They have requested that Mimi _____.

5. We only ask that your son _____.

# Punctuation

Punctuation is used to make text easier to read and to convey clear and specific meaning. It is used to divide words into grammatical units, like clauses within sentences. Punctuation marks consist of a set of standardized symbols: periods, commas, semicolons, colons, question marks, exclamation points, apostrophes, quotation marks, hyphens and dashes, and parentheses and brackets. The proper use of these symbols is governed by grammatical and stylistic guidelines.

## The period

A **period** is used to end a **declarative** sentence or **imperative** sentence. The period stands inside quotation marks.

> They are going to the mall.
> Hand me the book next to you, please.
> Finish your dinner so you can go to sleep.
> She said, "I'm not leaving my purse on the table unattended."

Periods are also often used with abbreviations and acronyms.

> Massachusetts Ave. begins in Dorchester.
> The U.S. and China are the countries most responsible for greenhouse gas emissions.

If a sentence ends with an abbreviation or acronym, no additional period is required.

> They will bring the dishes, serving pieces, flatware, etc.
> The train arrives at ten P.M.
> Their son recently received his B.S.

EXERCISE

23·1

*Add periods where needed.*

1. The city council requested that Gov Madison allocate more funds to the development of children's playgrounds

2. Richard told his parents, "I enjoy having dinner before eight o'clock, because it gives me enough time to finish my homework before going to sleep"

3. Meet them at Whole Foods for breakfast

4. Nathan said to his professor, "I can't be done with my paper by Monday"

5. I thanked Mrs Bronco for giving us a ride to school this morning

6. Sgt Pepper was called to the conference room for an important membership meeting

# The comma

A **comma** is used to separate two independent clauses joined by any of the following coordinating conjunctions: *and, but, for, or,* and *nor.*

> The men remained in the kitchen, and the women went out to the garden.
> We were supposed to go boating, but the storm changed our plans.
> Should we stay home tonight, or should we go out to dinner?

A comma is used to separate a dependent clause from the main clause that follows.

> Even though the concert was great, we had to leave early.
> When I was through with the dishes, I sat down with a glass of wine.

If the dependent clause follows the main clause, the comma is often not used.

> I sat down with a glass of wine when I was through with the dishes.

A comma is used to separate an introductory element from the main clause of a sentence.

> Running as fast as he could, Chris finished second in the marathon.
> Taken completely by surprise, the enemy was forced to surrender.

A comma is used after a wide range of introductory words, including *yes, no, oh,* and *well,* at the beginning of a sentence.

> No, I can't tell you why she left so suddenly.
> Well, they may stay in the guest room if they leave by tomorrow afternoon.

A comma is used to separate an apposite phrase from the rest of a sentence. An **apposition** is a word or phrase placed after another to provide additional information about it or to explain it.

> Erin likes that dress, which she bought at a Macy's sale, because it fits so well.
> We saw that blue car, the one that is parked right over there on the street, the last time we ate here.
> My game console, an Xbox, offers crystal clear graphics.

A comma is used to separate declarative elements from a clause that poses a question.

> She is depending on those grades, isn't she?
> That movie was beautiful, don't you think?

A comma is used to separate groups of numbers, the different elements of an address, and the date from the year. A comma ordinarily is not used to separate the name of a month from the year.

> Their twentieth wedding anniversary was on March 10, 2000.
> Barbara and I lived at 232 Lorraine Road, Austin, Texas for roughly ten years.
> He left South Korea in May 1977.

A comma is used to separate interrupting elements from the rest of a sentence.

> If Shawn writes more than 20 pages by the end of this weekend, and we doubt he will, he will treat himself to a smoothie.
> When John finishes his degree, which would be some kind of a miracle, he plans to start his own business.
> Karen won a prize in the lottery and, with any luck, will be able to pay off her debts.

A comma is used at the end of the greeting of a personal letter and at the end of the closing.

> Dear Mr. Mustar,
> Sincerely yours,

A comma is used to separate numbers composed of four or more digits (except for years).

> The company made more than $8,000,000 in the last fiscal year.
> We need 1,500 cubic yards of concrete for the parking lot.

A comma is sometimes used when the meaning of a sentence needs to be preserved and to avoid confusion.

> She asked me why I hadn't kissed her, and giggled.  (to make clear that it is *she* who giggled)

A comma is used to separate direct quotations from the rest of a sentence.

> Mr. Wilson told me, "There is no gain without some loss."
> The president always said, "To protect our freedom, I must be conservative."

A comma is used to separate the person or persons being addressed from the rest of the sentence.

> Ladies and gentlemen of the jury, may I have your attention?
> Jack, turn down the volume on the TV.

A comma is used to separate items in a series.

> We bought apples, plums, and a bushel of tomatoes.
> They hope to visit France, Germany, and the Netherlands.

EXERCISE
23·2

*For each sentence, explain the use of the comma(s).*

1. Although we got there on time, we missed the train.

2. She had lived at 6745 East Pinch Street, Austin, Texas since January 17, 1998.

3. I went to the concert, but I had forgotten the tickets.

4. The foundation gave $1,876,937 to the education council of Burundi.

5. Albert did his homework, as promised, and should not be failed.

6. Distinguished ladies and gentleman, it is with pride that I appear before you tonight.

7. She was fascinated by his gentle, polite, elegant ways.

EXERCISE
23·3

*Add commas where needed.*

1. Taylor asked "How are we supposed to cook this with no oven?"

2. She packed two blouses a black skirt and a new business suit.

3. According to the U.S. Census Bureau the world population reached 6500000000 on February 25 2006.

4. Dear Mrs. Dimple

5. The Persian Gulf War officially ended on February 28 1991.

6. They were so excited by the soccer game which went into three overtimes that they hardly noticed the afternoon go by.

7. Marie Catherine and Chris are all going to the theater together.

8. IBM not Apple will build a fast computer.

9. If you've never been to the craft show there will be selected sales and bargain bins.

10. She will be participating won't she?

11. Yes I think there is enough time for you to pick it up and get back home before dinner.

12. If I could get a nickel for every time he lies I would be a billionaire.

13. He had intended to stay home but he decided instead to go running.

# The semicolon

A **semicolon** is used to mark a break between independent clauses in the same sentence. It links clauses that are closely related.

> She has asked them to leave several times; they had a habit of overstaying their welcome.
> For the second time, he rescued a drowning child; his bravery is well known.

A semicolon is also used before conjunctive adverbs and transitional phrases that join independent clauses.

> They had been walking around the neighborhood for hours, looking for the lost dog; at the same time, they talked to neighbors they had never met before.
>
> The salesman let the man take the car for a drive; soon after, he had the eager buyer signing the purchase papers.

A semicolon is used to join independent clauses connected by a coordinating conjunction (*and, but, for, or, nor, so,* or *yet*) when at least one of the clauses contains a comma.

> It was time for the football team to take a break, drink some water, and stretch; but there were so many different exercises, and they had such a limited space, that they would need to be on break for too long to really stretch properly.

A semicolon is used to separate a series of elements from the rest of the sentence when at least one of the elements is long and contains commas. These elements can be phrases or clauses.

> In his analytical thesis on the Ninth Symphony, the author decided to include information about Beethoven's father, Johann, who was his first music teacher; Christian Gottlob Neefe, his most important teacher in Bonn; and Giulietta Guicciardi, his fiancée.

A semicolon is placed outside quotations marks.

> Sheryl told them, "You might be scared when you watch this movie"; still, I don't think it's scary enough to prevent you from watching it.

Semicolons are never used to join dependent to independent clauses.

EXERCISE
23·4

*Add semicolons where needed.*

1. The computers at my job have large monitors, loud speakers, CD burners, DVD players, and all sorts of other useful hardware are equipped with the most recent software and have the most sophisticated firewall.

2. Peter was amazed by the talent of the opposing team's poetry skills at the same time, he knew his team could win the poetry contest.

3. Greg was the first to run out of the burning house however, Elizabeth was the one who made it to a pay phone to call the fire department.

4. Each of us had enough time to get in the hotel's swimming pool nevertheless, we were all there on business.

5. There are moments when one needs to think about a situation calmly and for a long time likewise, there are moments when one needs to make decisions quickly and instinctively.

6. Gina said, "Let's work as a group" Peter said, "We should work individually instead" and Andrew said, "Let's split the team, and while some can work as a group, others can work individually."

7. Karen has been painting the kitchen for three hours all the while, she has been cooking and playing with the dogs.

# The colon

A **colon** connects clauses that are closely linked in meaning or topic. Typically, the second clause continues or develops the thought of the first clause, or it contains an illustration or explanation of a topic in the first clause. If a complete sentence follows a colon, the first word of that sentence should be capitalized.

> Bill has 20 paintings on his wall: Ten of them he painted himself.
> The dictator was overthrown: The cruelty of his methods and the corruption of his government were finally exposed.
> Everything in his life seemed to be coming apart and collapsing: his marriage, his career, his confidence in himself.
> The economic sustainability of Bangladesh depends on three factors: the production of tea and rice, the export of garments, and foreign investment.

A colon is sometimes used to introduce dialogue or formal statements. In this case, the first word after the colon is capitalized.

> Julien could not help himself when the teacher asked him what was wrong: "There is no reason for all of us to be punished because Fred won't stop acting silly in class!"
> If she wants my opinion, this is what I shall tell her: "You need to raise your own kids when they're that little and stop leaving them in day care."

A colon is used after the greeting in formal or business letters.

> Dear Mrs. Jackson:
> Dear Governor:

A colon is used to separate hours and minutes in statements of time.

> 8:15 A.M.
> 11:37 P.M.

EXERCISE
23·5

*Add colons where needed.*

1. She told me what her favorite colors were blue, red, and light olive green.

2. Dear Madam President

3. It is 530 A.M.; why are you calling me so early?

4. There are three main ingredients in a cake sugar, flour, and eggs.

5. It was time for the lawyer to make his closing statement "My client is an honest man, a hardworking man, a good husband, and he should not be sitting in this court today."

6. Nixon said "Looting and pillaging have nothing to do with civil rights. Starting riots to protest unfair treatment by the state is not the best of solutions."

7. John has five trophies on his bookshelf Four of them are from basketball tournaments.

8. The professor made an interesting statement during class "We have not yet addressed the topic of social revolutions, which is a key component of our present argument."

# The question mark

A **question mark** is used at the end of a sentence to signal a question; it can be a direct question, an interrogative series, or an expression of editorial doubt.

> When are you coming?
> Peter waved his hands while jumping up and down. What if they failed to see him?
> What do you think of his paintings? sculptures? drawings?
> Despite his participation in the 1934 riots (?), we do not know which organization
> he was marching with.

# The exclamation point

An **exclamation point** or **mark** is used to signal an interjection, which is often associated with fear, surprise, shock, excitement, or disbelief. An exclamation point can also be used instead of a question mark to indicate that the overall emotion of a question is surprise, not interrogation.

> That's amazing!
> Great!
> He stops short, shoots, and scores!
> Did they really believe we were that stupid!

EXERCISE
23·6

*Insert questions marks and exclamation points where needed.*

1. Are you serious

2. Get out of here now

3. What do you think of the president's decision to go to war his views on foreign policy his thoughts on the economy

4. Quickly What are you waiting for

5. Are you in a hurry

6. When were you going to tell me

7. Super

8. That's so cool

9. Do you think the corporation will apologize for unjustly firing those employees taking

   away their retirement not providing them with a severance package

10. Are you out of your mind

# The apostrophe

An **apostrophe** is used in one of two ways: to form a contraction (a shortened version of two words) or to express possession. Following are some common English contractions.

> cannot → **can't**
> do not → **don't**
> it is → **it's**
> what is → **what's**
> who is → **who's**

In the same way that the apostrophe is used to replace letters that have been omitted, it can also be used to indicate that numbers have been omitted.

> 1990 → **'90**
> 2008 → **'08**

The following examples illustrate the use of the apostrophe to express possession.

> **Damien's** car is really fast.
> **Rosie's** roses are so pretty.
> The roller skates are **Helen's**.
> Have the **employees'** paychecks come in yet?

When an apostrophe is used to indicate joint ownership, only the last word has the apostrophe.

> **My grandmother and grandfather's** paintings are in the attic.
> **Bill and Peter's** car dealership is at the next intersection.

If joint ownership is not involved, each party has an apostrophe.

> **Tim and Barbara's** pets  (*All the pets belong to both Tim and Barbara.*)
> **Tim's and Barbara's** pets  (*Tim has his pets, and Barbara has hers.*)

*It's* is a contraction of *it is,* whereas *its* is a possessive pronoun.

> **It's** the most complicated problem I've had to solve.
> **Its** art collection was lost in the fire.

## EXERCISE 23·7

*For each sentence, explain why the apostrophe is used (or not used).*

1. Paul's and Janet's painting techniques are very different.

_____

2. The cassettes were sent overseas by a company in Florida.

_____

3. It's time the dog had its walk.

_____

4. Wireless keyboards have been used since the 1990s.

_____

5. The Doors' second single was an instant hit.

_____

6. Peter and Margaret's car is navy blue.

_____


## EXERCISE 23·8

*Insert apostrophes where needed. If no apostrophe is needed, mark it with an X.*

1. The sergeants boots were always the shiniest of all.

2. She really likes that about the 80s.

3. A doctors quick intervention can save a life.

4. There are times when the UNs presence has prevented armed conflict.

5. Whos winning today?

6. Our planes took off at the same time.

7. By the 1940s, jazz was already becoming an important musical movement.

8. Natalies new bicycle is red and yellow.

9. The Cutlips cat wandered into our garage this morning.

10. Her mothers and fathers wills were drafted by the lawyer.

# Quotation marks

**Quotation marks** are used for the title of a short work, to indicate direct quotations, to indicate a part of a large work, and to emphasize certain, often ironic words. Quotation marks indicate the direct comments of a speaker or remarks taken from written material.

"The Raven" is the title of a poem written by Edgar Allan Poe. (TITLE OF A SHORT WORK)
Mark Twain first became known for his short story "The Celebrated Jumping Frog of Calaveras County." (TITLE OF A SHORT WORK)
She said, "There they go again," as the children raced back outside to play. (DIRECT QUOTATION)
In an article from last week's *Economist*, I read that "10% of the world's population controls 90% of the wealth." (DIRECT QUOTATION)
"When Business Mergers No Longer Work" was an article published in the *New Yorker*. (PART OF A LONGER WORK)
I agree, the theater play was so "entertaining" that I slept through most of it.
His latest painting is proof of "his creative skills" and worth every cent of the $20 he wants for it.

Single quotation marks are used to enclose a quotation within another quotation. The first quote is noted in the standard way, with double quotation marks, and the embedded quote is noted with single quotation marks.

In his speech, Charles brought up an interesting point: "If Adam Smith wrote that 'the subjects of every state ought to contribute towards the support of the government, as nearly as possible, in proportion to their respective abilities,' then why are people clamoring for a flat tax?"

EXERCISE
23·9

*Insert quotation marks where needed. If none are needed, mark it with an X.*

1. I met a woman who said she could make magic potions.

2. From what I hear, Joseph said the turning point in the novel is when Carlito tells his cousin, You should have never worked with Francisco in the first place; he's not to be trusted.

3. She read The Palm-Tree and was very moved by the poem.

4. What do you think of John Coltrane's tune My Favorite Things?

5. The morning newspaper mentioned that there might be snow tonight with a chance of hail and strong winds.

6. His father asked him, What would you like to do this summer, work or travel?

7. As Patrick walked away, she hesitated and then screamed, Will you go out with me?

8. The title of the book, How to Find Happiness Quickly, intrigued me.

9. We analyzed the play The Flies by Jean-Paul Sartre and his famous essay Americans and Their Myths.

10. The song Organ Donor is best qualified as groundbreaking.

11. The photographer encouraged the model by telling her, You're doing really well, but I want you to relax a little more. When the camera is pointed at you, just imagine someone is saying to you, You're the only one that can do this, and I want you to believe it!

# The hyphen and the dash

A **hyphen** is used to divide or syllabify words at the end of a line when the word runs over to the beginning of the next line. It also connects individual words to form a compound word.

Hyphens cannot be used to divide one-syllable words: *thought, through, weight,* and so on. Hyphens can be used to divide words of two or more syllables.

> fun-damental
> funda-mental
> fundamen-tal

If a word already contains a hyphen, it is generally syllabified using that hyphen.

> a **mid-life** crisis
> a **cross-cultural** conference

A number of everyday words and expressions are hyphenated: U.S. Social Security numbers (*666-86-3454*), telephone numbers (*555-342-4536*), and certain compound nouns (*two-step*) and adjectives (*two-way*). Following are examples of hyphenated everyday words.

> hard-driving
> long-winded
> out-of-pocket
> pitch-dark
> six-cycle
> twice-told
> Yves Saint-Laurent

> When dividing words at the end of a line, leave at least two letters at the end of the line and bring at least three letters down to the beginning of the next line.

A **dash** interrupts the flow of a sentence and sets a separate thought off from the rest of a sentence.

> If you find yourself in a dangerous situation, use the two Bs method—back off and breathe in—because otherwise you might panic.
> She was thinking of ways of running away—how could she have agreed to be part of this nonsense—but she was stuck.

EXERCISE
23·10

*Insert hyphens and dashes where needed.*

1. Eric could not figure out how to get out of the maze how silly and useless he felt!

2. The touchdown scored by the Patriots was an 83 yard play.

3. They were once considered wishy washy.

4. Carla was about to close the front door and thought to herself do I have everything I need in the bag?

5. The tight lipped receptionist told the reporters nothing.

6. She detests animal testing, so she never buys Yves Saint Laurent products.

7. Thirty two of the 52 figure skaters missed at least one of their jumps.

8. The Security Council voted against three crucial resolutions an armed attack, a forced embargo, and unified retaliation.

# Parentheses and brackets

**Parentheses** enclose explanatory material, supplemental material, or any added information that could clarify the text it refers to. They are placed at the beginning and end of the enclosed text.

> The museum demolition that began in 1993 (and ended in 1996) was a sad reminder of how suddenly historical buildings can be taken away.

Parentheses can be used in text references.

> The death toll of Hurricane Katrina was staggering (see Table 5.7).

Parentheses can be used to set off a list of elements.

> The green screen on your left indicates (1) the wind speed, (2) the outside temperature, (3) the atmospheric pressure, and (4) the humidity ratio.

**Brackets** enclose editorial comments and corrections.

> These painting copies [reproduced from the original artworks that burned in the fire of 1954] are listed as some of the most expensive art of the exposition.
> The students prefer Milton over him [Shakespeare].
> The president said, "The illiteracy level of our children are [sic] appalling."

Brackets can also be used to replace a set of parentheses within a set of parentheses.

> During his trial, Fidel Castro stated, "None of you are entitled to condemn, you'll see, history will absolve me!" (See Fidel Castro's speech "History Will Absolve Me" [October 16, 1953].)

EXERCISE
23·11

*Insert parentheses and brackets where needed.*

1. *The Skibby Chronicle* published anonymously in the 1530s but now believed to be the work of Poul Helgesen describes Danish history from 1047 to 1534.

2. As members of the book club, we had to read *The Stranger* Albert Camus 1913–1960 and discuss the novelist's concept of the absurd.

3. According to historical accounts, the first bridge over the Chattahoochee River there Columbus, Georgia was built by John Goodwin in 1832–1833.

4. They were told there was a heavy load of work that they would have to deal with during the semester: They would have to 1 take two three-hour exams, 2 read 13 books, and 3 write a 50-page essay.

5. Thomas Hart Benton 1888–1975 finished his famous *Indiana Murals* in 1932.

6. Some scholars argue that Michelangelo noted Italian painter and sculptor 1475–1564 was the quintessential Renaissance man.

# ·24· Capitalization, numbers, and italics

## Capitalization

The first word of a sentence is always capitalized.

> **John** hurried to the drugstore.
> **She** always traveled with too much luggage.
> **Have** you spent a lot of time abroad?
> **Sometimes**, I wish I were a rock star.
> **Wealthy** people are not always intelligent people.

Proper nouns are always capitalized. If the proper noun is the name of a nation, the corresponding nouns referring to the nation's people and language are also capitalized.

PROPER NAMES

Joanna, Laurie, Paul, Sebastian, Tyler Johnson

| COUNTRY | NATIONALITY | LANGUAGE |
| --- | --- | --- |
| Germany | German | German |
| Spain | Spaniard | Spanish |
| Korea | Korean | Korean |

Civil, military, religious, and professional titles, even when abbreviated, are capitalized when followed by a person's name.

> **Pope** Benedict XVI
> **President** Bill Clinton
> **Professor** Gibbons
> **Rabbi** Dahan
> **Dr.** Joanna Hughes
> **Ms.** Gloria Graham
> **Rev.** Lewis
> **Sir** Winston Churchill

When a person is addressed by his or her professional title, the title is capitalized.

> We beg you, **General**, to take our opinion into consideration.
> **Madam President**, I'd like to know what your budget proposal is.

The pronoun *I* is always capitalized. This is also true of the interjection *O*.

> Yesterday, **I** saw Megan in her wedding dress, and **O**, what a sight she was!

Geographical names are capitalized.

the Allegheny Mountains
the Champs-Élysées
the Danube
El Rastro
Madrid
the Mediterranean Sea
the Mississippi River
North Korea
the Pacific Ocean
the Sahara Desert
the Tai Po River
the Twin Cities
Washington, D.C.

Religions, holy books, believers (as a group), holy days, and terms that refer to deities are capitalized.

Hinduism, Hindu, Brahman, Shiva
Islam, Koran, Muslim, Ramadan, Allah
Christianity, the Bible, Christian, Christmas, God

Names of organizations, institutions, government agencies, companies, as well as their abbreviations, acronyms, and shorter versions of their names, are capitalized.

the ACLU
Alpha Delta Kappa
Boy Scouts of America
the Red Cross
the FCC
NYPD
UNESCO
IBM
the Rand Corp.
the Yanks

Days of the week, months of the year, and holidays are capitalized. The seasons, however, are not usually capitalized.

Sunday
Monday
April
October
Veterans Day
Thanksgiving
summer
winter

Historical documents, events, periods, and cultural movements are capitalized.

Declaration of Independence
Magna Carta
World War II
the Renaissance
Cubism

However, ideologies and related terms not used as part of a proper-noun phrase are not capitalized.

IDEOLOGIES   democracy, democrat, democratic; communism, communist
PROPER NOUNS   German Democratic Republic, Communist China

Names of trademarked merchandise are capitalized.

Adbusters
Adidas
Monopoly
Nike
Oreo
Post-it
Puffs
Velcro
Yahoo

Words derived from proper names are capitalized.

Machiavellian
Europeanization
Americanized

The titles of poems, songs, movies, books, plays, and essays are capitalized. Articles, conjunctions, and prepositions are not capitalized, unless they are the first word of the title. Prepositions are capitalized if they are the last word of the title.

"The Second Coming"
"Take the 'A' Train"
*The Motorcycle Diaries*
*The Grapes of Wrath*
*Love's Labour's Lost*
"How the Palestinian-Jewish Conflict Began"

The first word in quoted material is usually capitalized.

She turned around and screamed, "Is there anybody out there!"
A timid voice asked, "Is there more food, sir?"

The names of heavenly bodies, including the planets, are capitalized, but the words *earth, moon,* and *sun* are not.

Andromeda Galaxy
Milky Way
Scorpio
Jupiter

The **earth** was parched and cracked; the drought had done its work.
The **earth** is the third planet from the sun.

General compass directions are not capitalized unless they refer to specific geographical locations.

Lyon is **south** of Paris.
They walked in an **easterly** direction.
The red team represents the **West**.
They came from the **South**.
They came from the **Southern** states.

The names of man-made objects, such as bridges, planes, spacecraft, ships, roads, monuments, and buildings, are capitalized.

> the Brooklyn Bridge
> the *Spirit of St. Louis*
> *Apollo 13*
> the *Santa María*
> Interstate 35
> the Lincoln Memorial
> the Museum of Natural Science
> the Sears Tower

## EXERCISE
## 24·1

*Rewrite each sentence, using correct capitalization.*

1. teresa malcolm is president of the ford rotary club.

   _____

2. in three weeks, we will be traveling through france, switzerland, and spain.

   _____

   _____

3. the night sky was so clear we could see the entire moon, venus, and jupiter.

   _____

   _____

4. as soon as he got home, patrick felt like putting on his new adidas swimsuit.

   _____

   _____

5. the second world war lasted nearly six years.

   _____

6. the novel we bought at the airport was *the da vinci code.*

   _____

7. i visited the empire state building when i was in new york.

   _____

8. thelma and john saw the launch of the *uss enterprise.*

   _____

9. the naacp is a prominent organization based in the united states.

   _____

10. they told her, "we don't like the proposal you've written."

   _____

*Rewrite each sentence, using correct capitalization.*

1. marilyn is the president of the ladies of grace at her church.

   _____

2. some restaurants in los angeles serve americanized european food.

   _____

3. members of all faiths gathered on campus to protest, including christians, jews, muslims, and hindus.

   _____

   _____

4. "the red wheelbarrow" by william carlos williams is one of the most profound poems i've read.

   _____

   _____

5. they came from the eastern states in search of gold.

   _____

6. we read *of mice and men* last week for class.

   _____

7. the cia agent said he often works with fbi investigators, as well as with representatives of the faa.

   _____

   _____

8. a speaker from the national transportation safety board gave a presentation on the most common accidents that took place on interstate 66.

   _____

   _____

# Numbers

**Whole numbers** from one through ten are usually spelled out in sentences; whole numbers larger than ten are written as numerals. However, this is a style—not grammar—issue, and the main objective should be consistency.

> **Eight** in **ten** voters were disappointed.
> This hospital employs **437** nurses.

A number that begins a sentence is spelled out and capitalized.

> **Twenty-eight thousand** people crossed the border.

Very large numbers can be expressed in several ways.

**30,000** political prisoners
**30 thousand** political prisoners
**thirty thousand** political prisoners

Numbers used in business documents or in legal writing are often spelled out and written as numerals to avoid confusion.

The broker's profits are not to exceed **forty thousand (40,000)** dollars.

## Uses of numbers

Numbers can be used to express time, dates, and periods of time.

**3** P.M. ~ **3:00** P.M. ~ **three** o'clock in the afternoon
July **23, 1976**
the **seventeenth** century ~ the **17th** century
the **'80s** ~ the **eighties** ~ the **1980s**

Numbers are used in addresses.

**1949** Yucca Mountain Road
**1600** Liberal Lane
Chicago, IL **60601**

Numbers are used in decimals, percentages, pages and chapters of books, scenes in a play, temperature, geographic coordinates, money, and forms of identification.

**0.0987, 20.75**
**17** percent ~ **17%** ~ **seventeen** percent
page **34,** chapter **45**
Act **V,** Scene **III,** lines **108–110**
**36°** C ~ **36** degrees Celsius
latitude **45°** N
**$5.30** ~ **five** dollars and **thirty** cents
Queen Elizabeth **II,** Henry **VIII**
Channel **8**
Area **51**

EXERCISE
**24·3**

*Rewrite each sentence, using the numbers correctly. If the sentence is correct and no changes are required, mark an X in the blank.*

1. An important date to remember is November seventeen 1959.

_____

2. The city paid $ thirty-four point seven million to build the tower.

_____

3. It took 5 out of 9 members to reach a consensus.

_____

4. In Europe, the nineteen seventies were marked by social and political change.

_____

5. Turn to page one hundred and nine, which should be chapter twelve.

_____

6. The morning temperature was forty-seven degrees Fahrenheit, or 8 degrees Celsius.

_____

7. The address listed in the phone book was 3465 Milkway Avenue.

_____

8. They drove down Interstate thirty-four to the lake.

_____

9. The Second Battle of Bull Run was fought from August twenty-eight to thirty, eighteen sixty-two.

_____

# Italics

**Italics** are used to make a word or group of words stand out in order to give them emphasis.

> Notre Dame de Paris is an *amazing* cathedral.

Generally, a word processor is used to create italic text, but in handwriting, it is common to underline words that ordinarily would be italicized.

Italics are often used to indicate the titles of books, newspapers, magazines, plays, lengthy poems, comic strips, software, paintings, sculpture, movies, and genus/species references.

| | |
|---|---|
| *Gone with the Wind* | *InDesign CS3* |
| *The New York Times* | *Guernica* |
| *Science News* | *Venus de Milo* |
| *All's Well That Ends Well* | *When Harry Met Sally …* |
| *The Song of Hiawatha* | *Drosophila melanogaster* |
| *Doonesbury* | |

Italics are also used to set off foreign words adapted into English. Most of these words and phrases are still italicized, because they remain foreign to most English speakers.

| | |
|---|---|
| *coup de grâce* | *prix fixe* |
| *je ne sais quoi* | *pro bono* |
| *persona non grata* | *verboten* |

Some foreign words, however, are not italicized, because they have been integrated into English and are commonly used. This generally happens after widespread adoption and use by the mass media and the publishing industry. The following list includes some of these words.

| | | |
|---|---|---|
| bazaar | cuisine | ski |
| cappuccino | igloo | soprano |
| casino | karaoke | taffeta |
| chauffeur | rodeo | yogurt |

Italics are used to identify court cases.

*Brown v. Board of Education*
*Roe v. Wade*

Italics are used in algebraic expressions.

$X - Y = 23$

Italics are used for the names of spacecraft, satellites, and ships.

*Sputnik* was launched into orbit this morning from a base in Kazakh SSR.
Launched in 1959, *Vanguard 2* helped to map the shape of the earth.
Sink the *Bismarck*!

EXERCISE
24·4

*Rewrite each sentence, using correct capitalization and italicization. Also, rewrite numbers that are used incorrectly.*

1. We installed windows vista on our desktop today.

_____

2. Jason's spanish literature class read Miguel de Cervantes' Don Quixote.

_____

3. They reviewed the case of The People v. Robert Page Anderson for their law class.

_____

4. He invited ten of his closest friends, but more than ninety people showed up.

_____

5. Did you get a copy of the atlantic monthly?

_____

6. The lawyer working on Miller v. Wilson offered his services pro bono.

_____

7. The baton rouge advocate gave us information about visiting the garden district.

_____

8. The detective speculated about the criminal's modus operandi.

_____

# APPENDIX
# Review exercises

*Underline the entire auxiliary verb in each sentence.*

1. We have to go grocery shopping.

2. He has to be able to run five miles in less than half an hour.

3. He is able to speak Persian.

4. He should be working a lot harder if he wishes to pass the exam.

5. I had better see a dermatologist.

6. She is my friend, so I am going to have to tell her.

7. I am going to write a novel based on our family.

8. I had better be able to pass this driving test.

*Complete each sentence with the appropriate tense of the verb in parentheses.*

1. ADRIAN: Hi, Loretta. _____ (you + meet) my close friend Kerry?

   LORETTA: No, I don't believe I _____ (ever + have) the pleasure of making his acquaintance.

   ADRIAN: Well, let me introduce you!

2. BETH: Wait! What _____ (you + do)?

   ADRIAN: I _____ (try) to pull out whatever _____ (jam) the blender.

   BETH: You really should not _____ (put) your hand in there while

   it's still plugged in. You _____ (probably + hurt) yourself.

3. ADRIAN: There's Loretta.

   BETH: Where?

   ADRIAN: She _____ (sit) on that bench in the shade.

   BETH: Oh yes, I _____ (see) her now.

   She _____ (certainly + look) focused. Let's go bother her anyway.

4. KERRY: What _____ (be) wrong with Adrian?

   BETH: While he _____ (run), his shoelaces
   _____ (come) untied and he _____ (fall).

   KERRY: I _____ (not + believe) it! _____ (be)
   you serious?

   BETH: Yes. I'm not kidding you. I wish I _____ (be), but I'm not.

   KERRY: Poor Adrian, he _____ (seem) to _____
   (suffer) quite a bit too.

5. PAUL: _____ (you + take) an Economics component this semester?

   PATRICIA: No, I _____ (not + be).

   PAUL: _____ (you + ever + take) it?

   PATRICIA: Yes, I _____ (have).

   PAUL: When _____ (you + take) it?

   PATRICIA: In 2006.

   PAUL: Who _____ (teach) the class back then?

   PATRICIA: Dr. Bumshelgell.

   PAUL: I _____ (take) his class next semester. _____
   (be) he a good professor?

   PATRICIA: When I _____ (take) the class, he _____
   (be) very pleasant to work with. His class _____ (be) very difficult
   to pass, but it's well worth it.

6. DANIEL: I _____ (spend) some time in Prague last month.

   I _____ (never + be) there before.

   JESSE: What _____ (you + do) while you were there?

   DANIEL: My girlfriend and I _____ (drive) around, randomly stopping
   in places we _____ (think) looked interesting.

7. The weather _____ (be) terrible lately. It _____
   (rain) off and on for a whole week, and for two days the temperature
   _____ (drop) below ten degrees. It _____ (be)

in the low 40s right now. Just yesterday, the sun _____ (shine) and

the weather was as pleasant as can be. It almost seems like the weather

_____ (change) all the time, and one never

_____ (know) what to expect. At this point,

I _____ (be) ready for anything. When I wake up tomorrow

morning, maybe everything _____ (freeze).

8. BRIAN: I _____ (go) to a concert last night.

   GREGORY: _____ (it + be) any fun?

   BRIAN: I _____ (not + do) think so, but Patricia

   _____ (enjoy) it quite a bit.

   GREGORY: Who _____ (you + see)?

   BRIAN: Postal Service. I _____ (never + see) them perform live before.

   GREGORY: Oh! I _____ (see) them in concert, too.

   I _____ (go) to their concert when they were on tour a couple

   of years ago. I _____ (think) it _____ (be)

   a great show!

   BRIAN: Well, I _____ (not + think) so.

**EXERCISE**

**A·3**

*Underline the entire auxiliary verb in each sentence.*

1. It's the end of spring break, so Peter is going back to school next week.

2. We should open the window.

3. Allison is going to Austin next weekend.

4. We don't have to paint all the kitchen walls tonight.

5. Are we supposed to get there before nightfall?

6. Josh should have to pay for all the groceries.

7. Patricia is going to open a vintage record store next month.

8. Since last week, I have been running every morning.

9. Bureaucrats should be able to stay polite at all times.

10. He has been playing the drums all morning.

*In each sentence, the verb phrase contains a grammatical error or has an element missing. Rewrite the sentence correctly. There may be more than one correct answer.*

EXAMPLE     Mike has visit Philadelphia twice this past month.
            *Mike has visited Philadelphia twice this past month.*

1. Kenji been studying Portuguese.

2. Juan has live in Madrid for two years.

3. He has to came back to meet us here.

4. My father, Raoul, who studied Mathematics with my uncle, looking for a job.

5. After work, Anjali will going to the pub.

6. Last week, Mark was able to visited the president's office.

7. The soil is dry. They will not are able to plant vegetables there.

8. He doesn't likes his neighbors, because they're too noisy.

9. They didn't had any problems with the rental car.

10. I have been learned a lot since I began doing my exercises.

11. Are you think of buying another car soon?

12. She was visited many monuments when she was in Rome.

13. I didn't saw a single beautiful sunset.

14. He couldn't forgot her after the love affair.

15. He always attempting to catch the students cheating.

_____

16. Sometimes when I cross the street, I don't looked to see if a car is coming.

_____

17. I've thinking about it for a long time now.

_____

18. I feel my English grammar might improving.

_____

19. Mrs. Gilmore was sad, because her son had to went back to the front lines.

_____

20. All my friends can helps me become a better person.

_____

*Each sentence may have a noun or pronoun with an error in number. Write the corrected word in the blank. If the sentence is correct, mark an X in the blank.*

1. Some of us wanted to be talented musicians, and others wanted to be famous painter.

   _____

2. Good professors like graduate students to be outspoken in their class.

   _____

3. Each person should make up his or her own mind.

   _____

4. The 50 states of the United States all have their own law.

   _____

5. When he was elected, the president did what he had promised: He gave more power to the syndicates and more power to the worker themselves.

   _____

6. Talented people who come to Europe to study should then return to their countries to help improve their society.

   _____

7. I like to travel, because it helps me understand the custom of other countries.

   _____

## EXERCISE
## A·6

*Complete each sentence, supplying the missing auxiliary verb form.*

1. Sherlock will _____ meeting with his associate soon to discuss his theory.

2. Watson knew that he should _____ looking harder for clues.

3. The murderer could _____ tried to keep his prints off the doorknob.

4. They _____ captured the murderer by April 6.

5. He could not understand how the police might _____ found out where he lived.

6. Inspector Pretz pushed Jack into the prison cell, because he _____ not want to take any risks.

7. Now when I see Watson, I just tell him, "You are a genius!" because he could _____ found a way to solve the mystery.

8. When Sherlock Holmes _____ working on a case, he tries to use every little bit of information he can get his hands on.

## EXERCISE
## A·7

*Each item should be a complete, grammatical sentence. If it is, mark an X in the blank. If it contains an error, describe the error, and then write a correct, grammatical sentence based on the item.*

1. Teaching math to smart students.

_____

2. Listen!

_____

3. If you want to observe what is taking place.

_____

4. Last week, she began writing her new book.

_____

5. The European Union.

_____

6. I already ran three miles

_____

7. before I walked in, I rang the bell, hoping someone would open the door.

_____

8. Many different photographs in that dusty, black book.

_____

9. Has many children.

_____

10. Open the garage before you leave.

_____

11. The Panama Canal can be a dangerous zone.

_____

12. Writing complete sentences is easy.

_____

13. If your friend is a lawyer, doesn't have to worry about finding a job.

_____

14. Madrid it is the capital of Spain.

_____

15. Also, he very smart, quiet, and polite.

_____

EXERCISE
A·8

*Each item should be a complete, grammatical sentence. If it is, mark an X in the blank.
If it is not, write one or more correct sentences based on the item.*

EXAMPLE    To cook that much rice. She'll need more water.
           *To cook that much rice, she'll need more water.*

1. When I was younger. I thought the earth was flat.

_____

2. My ambition is to become a pilot.

_____

3. My favorite color was red. Because it reminded me of my sister.

_____

4. He hates horror movies. Because he gets scared immediately.

_____

5. Now I realize that dreaming is not enough.

_____

6. She is back it's the end of spring semester at UCLA.

_____

7. To paint this wall. You need a special brush.

_____

8. Elvis is over there. With Tupac and Biggie and they look happy.

_____

9. You will get a free subscription in addition you will receive a free towel. A matching bathrobe, a sticker, and a silver pen.

_____

_____

10. Once you have done all your stretching. Run for two miles or so.

_____

11. As soon as you get there, make sure you take a right.

_____

12. When the water is boiling. Put the pasta in the pot.

_____

13. After the sun comes up can begin hiking up the mountain.

_____

EXERCISE
A·9

*Complete each sentence with an appropriate form of the verb in parentheses.*

EXAMPLE    I hope that Catherine _____drives_____ (drive) carefully, because the roads are slippery.

1. I recommend that Pablo _____ (promote) to a managerial position.

2. We demand that you _____ (give) us the location of the treasure.

3. She requested that we not _____ (knock) on her door after midnight.

4. Mrs. Taylor insists that he _____ (be) careful with his new watch.

5. It was such a sunny day outside that my mom suggested we _____ (have) lunch in the park.

6. It is essential that hate crimes _____ (study) and eventually

   _____ (stop).

7. I request that I _____ (allow) to leave the room.

8. The students recommended that the finals _____ (postpone) until the end of summer.

9. The plastic surgeon requested that he _____ (remain) in his house until the infection has healed.

10. He insisted that the puppy _____ (name) after his dead cat.

11. Their coach recommended that they _____ (take) a week off.

12. I suggest that all citizens _____ (write) a letter to the president.

13. It is crucial that I _____ (meet) with you tomorrow.

14. It is essential that he _____ (talk) to the professor about his assignment.

15. It is necessary that all of you _____ (join) him at five o'clock sharp.

16. The theater director insisted that his stage _____ (be) perfect.

17. It is very important that no one _____ (admit) backstage without a pass.

18. It is essential that they _____ (not + be) late to their meeting.

19. It is essential that he _____ (return) home immediately.

20. She specifically asked that I _____ (not + tell) anyone about the treasure.

EXERCISE
A·10

*Rewrite each sentence, correcting the error in subject-verb agreement.*

1. The private and public sectors in Africa needs to work closely together.

_____

_____

2. It is undeniable that armed conflict make things worse.

_____

3. They sit on the bench and feel that the judge condemn them for no apparent reason.

_____

_____

4. Many families in this area who doesn't own houses feels that they should get interest-free loans.

_____

_____

*Complete each passive sentence with the correct form of one of the verbs listed below.*

| | | | |
|---|---|---|---|
| build | expect | offer | spell |
| cause | frighten | order | surprise |
| confuse | invent | report | surround |
| divide | kill | schedule | wear |

EXAMPLE    An island ___*is surrounded*___ by water.

1. A necklace _____ around your neck.

2. The telephone _____ by the American scientist Alexander Graham Bell.

3. Is *sitting* really _____ with a double *t*?

4. Even though it took almost 20 years, the bridge _____ by next month.

5. I doubt the train will be coming in late. The monitor announced that it

   _____ to arrive on time.

6. I still can't understand the math problem. Yesterday in class, I _____ by the professor's explanation.

7. The children _____ in the middle of the night, because a squirrel managed to get inside their tent. They thought it was a monster.

8. Last week, she _____ a job at a local record store, but she had already decided to work as a waitress.

9. In spite of his knee injury, he _____ to play in the championship game.

10. The plane crash _____ in the newspapers last week.

11. They read about the hunter who _____ by the wild animal.

12. He enlisted in the army, but he _____ to return home because of a back injury.

13. Nathalie's house burned down. The fire _____ by lightning.

14. The team is too big, so it _____ into two smaller teams.

*Rewrite each sentence, correcting the grammatical error(s), if any. If the sentence is correct, mark an X in the blank.*

1. When we get older, you can do a lot of thing.

_____

2. Pedro ate a few piece of cheese with his enchilada.

_____

3. He read some book at the public library before they closed.

_____

4. Last year, I gave him *Star Wars* and *Indiana Jones* for Christmas, but I don't know
   if he ever watched those movie.

_____

_____

5. There are too many person in this car.

_____

6. My little sister is only three year old, but she seems older.

_____

7. We had not been to Portugal in six year.

_____

8. He is an intelligent and gifted 30-year-old actor.

_____

9. If you want to form your own opinion, you should read many news articles and watch
   many kind of documentaries.

_____

_____

10. In addition to the art gallery, there are a lot of beautiful place to visit.

_____

*Rewrite each sentence, correcting the grammatical error(s).*

1. She will going to Dallas to visit her brother.

_____

2. Patrick has know me since I was six years old.

_____

3. He been living in Lisbon for years but we still keeping in touch via e-mail.

_____

4. When I get to Peter's house, he will have to opens the front door.

_____

5. I soon noticed that Paul didn't drove very well. Among other things, he didn't respected the speed limit on the highways.

_____

_____

6. Paul knows that he should taking driving classes.

_____

7. If he were move back home he could helped his mom more, and he could to take care of her on a daily basis.

_____

_____

8. Vanessa should to do her shopping at Trader Joe's.

_____

9. I taking the GRE next month and I am quite nervous.

_____

_____

EXERCISE
A·14

*Rewrite each sentence, correcting the grammatical error(s), if any. If the sentence is correct, mark an X in the blank.*

1. In terms of transportation, cars are a basic parts of modern life.

_____

2. The automobile have made it possible for people to travel many mile from their home.

_____

3. Research has made great progress in the field of microbiology.

_____

4. Students study more than they used to, and learn about more thing than they used to.

_____

5. Life expectancy is much greater than it was a hundred year ago.

_____

*Rewrite each sentence, correcting the grammatical error(s), if any. If the sentence is correct, mark an X in the blank.*

1. The ten districts in this city has decided to build more modern-looking buildings.

   _____

2. Some cities in Argentina surprise tourists with its architecture.

   _____

3. Often, the term "third-world country" make people think of crime and poverty.

   _____

4. Technology has been crucial in modern society.

   _____

5. The graduate courses are very difficult; you feel like everyone else understand and you don't.

   _____

   _____

6. Study a lot, and you will get many of the answer right.

   _____

7. If a student don't understand the answer to his or her question, he or she should feels comfortable enough to ask again.

   _____

   _____

8. All students have to take the two part of the exam.

   _____

9. These drill cannot prove the ability of the nurses, because the nurses simply executes certain emergency procedures.

   _____

   _____

10. There are two kind of people in this company: honest persons and greedy persons.

    _____

11. There are many problem at my office, but one problem is the lack of motivation.

    _____

12. Any person whose parents are seriously sick worry about their health.

    _____

13. You can find many kind of people working in our offices.

    _____

14. Italian ice cream are so delicious. I'm pretty sure you'll like it.

_____

15. When I first came to this hotel, I didn't like the food, but now I like them very much.

_____

16. That was the first time I bought my own furniture. I enjoyed picking them out, and I felt like an adult.

_____

17. The people who shares my apartment are friendly, but they're messy.

_____

18. There are six freshly planted tree on my street.

_____

19. If you drive when you're too tired, he might cause an accident.

_____

20. I left my wallet and my keys on the counter. When I came back, I couldn't find it anymore.

_____

21. Everyone want to be successful and be in good healths.

_____

22. Count the money again before you put them in the envelope.

_____

23. Every people should help improve their neighborhood.

_____

EXERCISE
A·16

_Rewrite each sentence, correcting the grammatical error(s), if any. If the sentence is correct, mark an X in the blank._

1. My mother never forgets to put her house keys in her purse before she leaves the house.

_____

_____

2. Christine enjoys walking along the river. She likes that he's so peaceful.

_____

3. My boyfriend's mother is an attorney. He works for important people.

_____

4. If you want to purchase gloves, you can buy them online.

_____

5. He needed a coffee table and a couch, but he decided he could live without it.

_____

6. My cousins are all younger than I, but she is taller than I am.

_____

7. Japan is a small country. They have a long history.

_____

8. Many person in the world are learning English. This person wants to improve his language skills and get a better job.

_____

_____

9. If the tourists go to Puerto Rico, you should visit Old San Juan. You ought to try the food too, because they're delicious.

_____

_____

10. All his ideas comes from dreams, and he tries to make this dream reality.

_____

11. Mrs. Hutchinson put his jacket back on.

_____

EXERCISE
A·17

*Rewrite each sentence, correcting the grammatical error(s).*

1. This government has been running by Cardinal Richelieu since 1626.

_____

2. I'm quite exciting to see her again.

_____

3. I am so happy. Finally, I was pass the exam.

_____

4. They're not sure if the problem will be work out by tomorrow.

_____

5. I'm interesting in advance technology.

_____

6. The other colors have to be change.

   _____

7. We need to love someone and be love.

   _____

8. This question can be decide by taking into account all the information we've gathered.

   _____

9. I like the people there, because they're very educate.

   _____

10. I like the way math is teaching in her class.

    _____

11. This store is locate on the third floor of the mall.

    _____

EXERCISE
A·18

*Complete each sentence with an appropriate active- or passive-voice form of the verb in parentheses.*

1. Before Paul graduated last December, he _____ (offer) a position with a consulting firm.

2. I'm sorry I'm so late. I _____ (hold up) in traffic.

   It _____ (take) me an hour to get here instead of half an hour.

3. According to a recent survey, out of every euro a German spends on groceries, 30 cents

   _____ (spend) on fruits and vegetables.

4. I was supposed to take my math test yesterday, but I _____

   (not + admit) into the testing room, because they _____

   (already + begin) the test.

5. Only two of us _____ (work) in the laboratory this morning when

   the explosion _____ (occur).

6. It's ten o'clock, so the mail should be here soon. The mailman _____ (generally + deliver) our mail before noon.

7. According to the cover of *The Economist*, solar energy _____ (use) extensively by the end of this century.

8. Paul _____ (study) Spanish here for the last two years. His spoken

   Spanish _____ (finally + get) better, but he still needs to improve

   his spelling.

9. Right now, tickets to the concert _____ (sell) at the counter. If you want to go to the concert, you should hurry up and buy some tickets before it's too late.

10. John is a hero. His name will go down in history. He _____ (never + forget).

11. When you _____ (arrive) at the bus station tomorrow morning,

you _____ (meet) by my sister. She _____ (wear) a red shirt and a black skirt. She _____ (stand) near the main

entrance. I'm sure you will be able to find her.

12. Today _____ (be) a terrible day. First, I _____ (lose) my car keys. Then, I _____ (drop) my glasses on the floor

while I _____ (walk) and they _____ (break).

Finally, my car _____ (steal).

EXERCISE
## A·19

*Complete each sentence with an appropriate active- or passive-voice form of the verb in parentheses.*

1. The Amazon rainforest needs to be protected, because almost 20 percent of the planet's

oxygen _____ (produce) there.

2. Did you see that terrible car accident on the highway? Several of my friends

_____ (see) it, including one who _____

(interview) by a police officer.

3. In Europe, certain prices _____ (control) by the government.

Other prices _____ (determine) by the market.

4. I am so mad! Earlier today, the wind _____ (blow) my cap

off. I tried to catch it, because it was autographed by A-Rod and it

_____ (cost) a lot of money.

5. Right now, Alice is in the hospital. She _____ (treat) for a really
bad sunburn on her forehead.

6. Frostbite occurs when the skin _____ (expose) to extremely cold

weather. It mostly _____ (affect) hands, feet, noses, and ears.

7. Some researchers claim that Napoleon did not die of natural causes, but that he

_____ (poison) instead.

8. The government used to finance this school. Today, it _____
(support) by the generous donations of alumni.

9. Charles was demoted this morning. He _____ (tell) that he was being relieved of his duties as general manager, because he wasn't making enough money for the company.

10. The game _____ (probably + lose) by the opposing team tomorrow. We're a lot better than they are.

11. In 1989, photographs of Neptune _____ (send) back to earth by *Voyager 2*.

12. The World Health Organization hopes that a human vaccine for Ebola

_____ (develop) soon. Vaccines _____

(already + test) successfully on monkeys.

# Answer key

## 1 The sentence

**1·1** *Answers may vary.*
1. They were eating an Italian specialty.
2. They have worked in Austin for two years.
3. We purchased it last week.
4. The salad is awful.
5. It looks comfortable.
6. Mrs. Robinson went to the theater.

**1·2**
1. Children
2. Water
3. Prague
4. The furry, clean, calm cat
5. The furry, clean, calm, black cat
6. The furry, clean, calm, black cat with a scar
7. The big, ugly, dirty, brown bear with long ears and large claws
8. She
9. Peter
10. Lending money and giving too much advice

**1·3**
1. The big, brown dog sitting in the shade, is
2. I, drink
3. Saul, ordered
4. The youth hostels we stayed in while we were in Budapest, weren't
5. My professor, was
6. her father, is
7. presidential elections, will be held
8. the people who were sitting in the front row, got up

**1·4** *Answers may vary.*
1. After work
2. strange
3. never
4. Last week, new black
5. seriously
6. In winter, usually
7. younger, beautifully
8. quietly
9. horrible, in the city
10. rather

## 2 The verb phrase

**2·1**
1. doesn't go
2. goes
3. is heading out
4. washes
5. is going
6. has traveled
7. has been practicing
8. has to be
9. goes
10. had visited
11. is going to travel

| 2·2 | 1. does | 5. has |
|-----|---------|--------|
|     | 2. is   | 6. should |
|     | 3. is   | 7. has to |
|     | 4. has  |        |

**2·3**

1. James is trying on a pair of pants.
   James has tried on a pair of pants.
   James should try on a pair of pants.
2. I am living on about a hundred dollars a week.
   I have lived on about a hundred dollars a week.
   I should live on about a hundred dollars a week.
3. Father is scolding the children.
   Father has scolded the children.
   Father should scold the children.
4. Is she working hard?
   Has she worked hard?
   Should she work hard?
5. The conductor is waiting on the platform.
   The conductor has waited on the platform.
   The conductor should wait on the platform.

# 3   The verb

**3·1**

*Answers may vary.*

| 1. seemed OR sounded | 5. is OR tastes |
|----------------------|-----------------|
| 2. looks             | 6. sounds       |
| 3. appear OR seem OR look | 7. is OR feels |
| 4. are               |                 |

**3·2**

1. I studied mathematics.
   I have studied mathematics.
   I had studied mathematics.
   I will study mathematics.
   I will have studied mathematics.
2. Tom was going to Iraq.
   Tom has been going to Iraq.
   Tom had been going to Iraq.
   Tom will be going to Iraq.
   Tom will have been going to Iraq.
3. Anna came along.
   Anna has come along.
   Anna had come along.
   Anna will come along.
   Anna will have come along.
4. They were driving to Arizona.
   They have been driving to Arizona.
   They had been driving to Arizona.
   They will be driving to Arizona.
   They will have been driving to Arizona.

**3·3**

1. Why does he run so fast?
2. The boys were swimming across the river.
3. The hungry campers have been eating the hot dogs.
4. I won't go to work today.
5. The old woman was being very nice to me.
6. My uncle has been singing in a chorus.
7. Will you be driving your dad's new car?
8. I thought about you.
9. We had been shopping there.
10. We camped on the side of a hill.

# 4 The progressive tenses

**4·1** *Answers may vary.*
1. I heard a loud noise
2. the accident took place
3. the electricity suddenly went off
4. the first two guests arrived early
5. The baby was being put to bed
6. I was looking for the light switch
7. I was playing volleyball with my son
8. Their car was speeding down the highway
9. I was sleeping in the hammock
10. I was just window-shopping

**4·2**
1. While they were opening their Christmas gifts, the Christmas tree fell over.
2. While Tom was swimming in the pool, his little brother fell in the water.
3. While she was speaking with the letter carrier, a taxi pulled up in front of the house.
4. While Ms. Howard was lecturing her class, her cell phone rang.
5. While the boys were playing checkers on the floor, the cat jumped into the middle of their game.

**4·3**
1. washes
2. eats, is eating
3. am trying
4. am still waiting
5. is shining
6. turns on, stays on
7. is hailing
8. is not playing
9. coaches, trains
10. attends, plays

**4·4**
1. called, was not, was visiting
2. heard, was
3. was shining, was blowing OR blew, were running OR ran
4. were joking, entered, stopped, pretended, were doing
5. opened, found
6. was organizing, dusted
7. preferred
8. was telling, fell, closed, walked
9. was running, caught, broke

**4·5**
1. arrive, will be waiting
2. will be sleeping, will be climbing, will be thinking
3. will be staying
4. is, will be raining
5. will be using
6. will be staying, am

# 5 The perfect tenses

**5·1**
1. has given
2. have smoked
3. have known
4. have never seen
5. felt
6. have already annoyed, got
7. has been
8. landed
9. broke

**5·2**
1. I have never fed
2. I have never read
3. I have never wrecked
4. I have never understood

5. I have never thought
6. I have never built
7. I have never flown
8. I have never held
9. I have never slept
10. I have never traveled
11. I have never taught
12. I have never voted
13. I have never listened
14. I have never caught
15. I have never made
16. I have never won
17. I have never sent
18. I have never eaten
19. I have never stolen
20. I have never fallen
21. I have never brought
22. I have never forgotten
23. I have never drunk

**5·3** *Answers may vary.*
1. the 17th of February, two days ago, the 15th of February, two days
2. in 1996, 12 years, 1996
3. 8, 2000, eight years, 2000
4. the 12th of March, on the 15th of December, December, almost three months

**5·4**
1. have made
2. has advanced
3. has changed, were, have become, were
4. has gotten, has also gotten, have become
5. had, went, talked
6. have you learned, began
7. have you met, have already met
8. have never tasted
9. Have you ever met
10. have already taken, failed, took
11. have you gone, have been, have never been, were you, also visited, took, you visited, were, had, have always wanted, have not had, went, have not traveled

**5·5**
1. Pedro
2. Mr. Prince
3. Tyler
4. Lucas
5. Lucy
6. Paul
7. Bertrand
8. Alicia
9. Kenji's uncle

**5·6**
1. was, had stopped
2. left, had collected, had recorded
3. had already given, got, had also handed out
4. felt, had taken OR took, had given OR gave
5. had been OR was, became
6. locked, walked out, had taken, forgot OR had forgotten
7. had been, made, had blocked out

**5·7**
1. ran, had not seen, recognized, had changed, had lost
2. had already occupied, bought, made
3. had never seen, visited
4. roamed, had become, evolved
5. had already begun, got, sat down, tried

**5·8**
   1. get, will already have left OR will have already left
   2. have been, had been, will have been
   3. will have been
   4. will have suffered, retires
   5. will have been running (and) swimming OR will have run (and) swum
   6. will have taken
   7. got, had already arrived
   8. have been walking OR have walked, had been walking OR had walked, will have been walking OR will have walked
   9. will have lived
  10. will have traveled OR will have been traveling

**5·9**
   1. goes, will meet, meets, will have watched
   2. has read, is reading, has been reading, intends, has read, has ever read
   3. began, has not finished, is reading
   4. are taking, fell, have been sleeping OR have slept, will sleep
   5. had already eaten, left, usually tries, heads out, do not eat, go, get, will try, go, will eat
   6. is studying, is also taking, begin
   7. went, wanted
   8. attends OR is attending
   9. locked, came, got, was mixing, uses, had been working OR had worked

**5·10**
   1. was, has not, need, do not have, do not know, do you need, will pay, takes or has taken
   2. is not, called, gets, am sitting OR will be sitting, studying
   3. sat, began, was sitting, asked, tried, was, did, was talking, sat, felt OR had felt, raised, asked
   4. was lying OR lay, heard, got, looked, opened, had just left, had taken off
   5. will take OR am taking, am really looking, will go, leave, will go, studies OR is studying, has been living, knows, has promised, am staying OR stay, have never been, have always wanted

**5·11**
| | |
|---|---|
| 1. verb | 4. auxiliary verb |
| 2. auxiliary verb | 5. verb |
| 3. verb | 6. auxiliary verb |

# 6   Modal auxiliaries

**6·1**
| | |
|---|---|
| 1. may | 6. can |
| 2. should OR may | 7. can |
| 3. might | 8. could |
| 4. Should | 9. may |
| 5. would | 10. should |

**6·2**   *Answers may vary.*
   1. borrow my truck any time
   2. like to become a ballerina
   3. leave for home before the storm begins
   4. have a close look at those worn-out tires
   5. train well for the triathlon
   6. stop by for a visit tomorrow
   7. turn down that radio
   8. drink so much

**6·3**
| | |
|---|---|
| 1. should | 9. must |
| 2. must | 10. must |
| 3. should | 11. must |
| 4. should | 12. should |
| 5. must | 13. must |
| 6. must | 14. should |
| 7. should | 15. should |
| 8. should | 16. must |

**6·4**
| | |
|---|---|
| 1. a | 4. a |
| 2. b | 5. b |
| 3. b | 6. a |

**6·5**
1. I shouldn't have gone to a movie.
2. I should have studied.
3. I shouldn't have played video games.
4. I should have looked it up in the dictionary.
5. I shouldn't have left the window open.
6. I shouldn't have turned off the fan.
7. I shouldn't have spent all my money while I was on vacation.
8. I should have gone grocery shopping.
9. I shouldn't have left my coat at home.
10. I shouldn't have lied to her.
11. I should have had coffee this morning.
12. I shouldn't have eaten all the ice cream.

**6·6**
1. do not have to
2. must not
3. does not have to
4. must not
5. must not
6. must not
7. do not have to
8. does not have to
9. do not have to
10. must not
11. does not have to
12. do not have to, must not
13. must not
14. do not have to
15. do not have to

**6·7**
1. You are to keep off the grass.
2. You are not to eat or drink inside.
3. You are to move to the rear of the plane.
4. You are not to feed the monkeys.
5. You are not to smoke.
6. You are not to allow visitors on board.
7. You are not to litter.
8. You are not to use the elevator in case of fire.

**6·8**
1. Can
2. May
3. Will
4. Shall
5. Can
6. Will
7. shall

**6·9**
1. a
2. b
3. a
4. a
5. a
6. b
7. b

# 7 The progressive forms of modal auxiliaries

**7·1**
1. must have been kidding
2. must be playing
3. should be studying
4. may be staying, might be staying
5. may have been kidding
6. must be raining
7. may be jogging
8. must be burning
9. could be riding, may be walking
10. must have been climbing

**7·2**
1. is
2. X
3. X
4. X, are
5. am
6. X
7. are
8. X
9. were
10. am
11. is
12. is, am

**7·3**
1. used to be, would open
2. used to be
3. would ask, would never let
4. would begin
5. used to be, would get together, would go, used to drink
6. used to be, would make up, would not help
7. used to be, would start, would have
8. would take
9. would walk
10. would swim, would dry out, would get ready, would hike
11. used to live, would always smile, would say, would clear

# 8 The auxiliary verb *do*

**8·1**
1. Do they come here?, Where do they come?
2. Did she stay there?, Where did she stay?
3. Did his airplane land in the morning?, Where did his airplane land in the morning?
4. Did the package arrive?, Where did the package arrive?
5. Does Robert live there?, Where does Robert live?

**8·2**
1. I do not own any black-and-white movies.
2. I do not have any problems with my computer.
3. We do not have any time to waste.
4. I did not see anyone I know (OR knew).
5. I do not need any help with my homework.
6. I do not trust any of you.
7. I do not trust anyone.

**8·3**
1. Do the girls need some help?, Don't the girls need some help?
2. Does she have a job in a bakery?, Doesn't she have a job in a bakery?
3. Did Bob see somebody in the shadows?, Didn't Bob see somebody in the shadows?
4. Do you like hot tea?, Don't you like hot tea?

**8·4**
1. verb
2. auxiliary verb
3. verb
4. auxiliary verb
5. verb
6. auxiliary verb

# 9 The passive voice

**9·1**
1. P
2. P
3. P
4. A
5. A
6. A
7. P
8. P
9. A

**9·2**
1. A hundred dollars was found by Maria.
2. The Preamble to the Constitution will be memorized by the students.
3. Were the tickets purchased by you?
4. Some ancient ruins have been discovered by them.
5. The room is being measured by Bill.

**9·3**
1. A thousand cars were manufactured at that plant.
2. Theories about that are being developed.
3. That painting will be bought today.
4. The opening of the new store has been postponed.
5. His work is not respected.

**9·4**
1. A new design for the logo has been suggested by Kevin.
2. The formula is going to be explained by the professor.
3. People at the bar are served by bartenders.
4. A speech is being prepared by Noam Chomsky.
5. Marie will be invited to the party by Alex.
6. The novel *American Gods* was written by Neil Gaiman.

**9·5**
1. will have been
2. is
3. is being
4. has been
5. is going to be
6. will be
7. had been

**9·6**
1. Every professional school in New York teaches technical skills.
2. TF1 is broadcasting the ping-pong tournament.
3. X
4. Keats wrote this poem. García Lorca wrote the other one.
5. X, Later, Arabs produced paper in Baghdad.
6. X
7. X

**9·7**
1. My purse was stolen by someone.
2. X
3. My fork was borrowed by Gabriel at lunch.
4. This antique sewing machine was made in 1834 by someone.
5. X
6. The plants were being watered by Steve when I walked into the garden this morning.
7. The president is going to be judged by the jury on the basis of his testimony.
8. When was the atomic bomb invented by America?
9. X
10. Is a reunion being organized by Maureen this week?
11. The Bible has been translated into many languages by professionals.

# 10 The passive form of modal auxiliaries

**10·1**
1. should be told
2. should have been driven
3. should clean OR should have cleaned
4. must be kept
5. couldn't be convinced
6. couldn't open
7. may be offered
8. may not offer
9. may have already been offered
10. may have already hired
11. must have been surprised
12. should have been sent
13. should be sent
14. had better clean
15. had better be cleaned
16. has to return OR will have to return
17. have to be returned OR will have to be returned OR had to be returned
18. ought to be divided
19. ought to have been divided

**10·2**   *Answers may vary.*
1. may be
2. can be seen
3. must be put
4. should not get
5. should not be encouraged
6. ought to be postponed
7. might be misunderstood
8. can't be explained
9. must be married
10. must have been left
11. will be displeased
12. has to be pushed
13. should be built
14. ought to be saved
15. has to be done
16. should be elected

# 11   The stative passive

**11·1**
1. disappointed
2. exciting
3. interested
4. gratifying
5. confusing
6. confused
7. excited
8. excited

**11·2**
1. is broken
2. is closed
3. was closed
4. is made
5. is shut
6. are bent, are folded
7. is finished
8. are turned
9. is not crowded
10. is hidden
11. is torn
12. are gone
13. is set, are finished, are lit
14. is made, is vacuumed, are washed
15. was stuck
16. is stuck

**11·3**
1. scheduled
2. is, crowded
3. am lost
4. am exhausted
5. am confused
6. is turned off
7. is insured
8. is stuck
9. are divorced
10. is gone
11. are, qualified
12. am married
13. is spoiled
14. is blocked
15. is located
16. Is, plugged in
17. is, done

**11·4**
1. is composed of
2. is interested in
3. is accustomed to
4. is scared of
5. am satisfied with

6. are covered with
7. are opposed to
8. is finished with
9. is married to
10. am, acquainted with
11. is tired of
12. Are, related to
13. is dedicated to
14. are disappointed with
15. am scared of
16. is dedicated to
17. are devoted to
18. is dressed in

# 12 Past participles with *get*

**12·1** *Answers may vary.*
1. No one is getting hired, because the company will go out of business.
2. Larry was getting annoyed, because the dog would not stop barking.
3. His pay is getting increased, because he did a great job on the project.
4. Younger candidates are getting elected, because the people want change.
5. He was getting fingerprinted when the police found the real culprit.

**12·2**
1. am getting tired
2. are, getting married
3. get dressed
4. got lost
5. got hurt
6. got tired
7. get accustomed
8. am getting worried
9. got confused
10. get upset
11. get done
12. get bored
13. got depressed
14. get packed
15. get paid
16. got hired, got fired
17. didn't get finished
18. got engaged, got married, got divorced

# 13 Participial adjectives

**13·1**
1. sleeping, slept
2. inventing, invented
3. losing, lost
4. destroying, destroyed
5. comparing, compared
6. reporting, reported
7. endangering, endangered
8. making, made
9. stealing, stolen
10. slaying, slain

**13·2**   *Answers may vary.*
1. It is an entertained group of children.
2. He/She is an entertaining circus clown.
3. This is a boring class.
4. They are bored students.
5. This is a frightening accident.
6. She is a frightened woman.
7. She was a surprised girl.
8. It was a loud and surprising noise.
9. It was hard and exhausting work.
10. They were exhausted men.

**13·3**
1. borrowed
2. terrified
3. terrifying
4. gratifying
5. stolen
6. embarrassing
7. damaging
8. damaged
9. crowded
10. frozen
11. injured
12. lasting
13. locked
14. deserted

# 14   Subject-verb agreement

**14·1**
1. are
2. writes
3. were
4. are
5. wakes
6. like
7. were
8. Do
9. were
10. is

**14·2**
1. were running
2. doesn't work
3. has
4. are
5. is screaming OR was screaming

**14·3**
1. am
2. are
3. are
4. are
5. is
6. is
7. is
8. was
9. were
10. were
11. were
12. was
13. was
14. was
15. was

**14·4**
1. is
2. has
3. is
4. are
5. are
6. belongs
7. are
8. are
9. is
10. is
11. is OR are, are
12. are
13. is
14. is
15. Do
16. Do
17. were
18. was
19. Do
20. is
21. is

**14·5**
1. are
2. is
3. are
4. isn't
5. is
6. aren't
7. are
8. isn't
9. is
10. are

| 14·6 | 1. is | 9. do |
|---|---|---|
| | 2. is | 10. are |
| | 3. is | 11. like |
| | 4. is | 12. is |
| | 5. tries | 13. fear |
| | 6. is | 14. are |
| | 7. is | 15. depends |
| | 8. is | 16. have |

| 14·7 | 1. Are | 13. is |
|---|---|---|
| | 2. are | 14. is |
| | 3. are | 15. provides |
| | 4. is | 16. violates |
| | 5. Do | 17. is |
| | 6. Does | 18. plan |
| | 7. is | 19. is |
| | 8. is | 20. is |
| | 9. makes | 21. are |
| | 10. keeps | 22. are |
| | 11. are | 23. is |
| | 12. knocks | 24. is |

14·8
1. Mark and Pamela
2. Manhattan
3. People
4. cars

14·9
1. was
2. is
3. talk
4. are
5. were

# 15 Agreement with nouns

| 15·1 | 1. They were | 7. They |
|---|---|---|
| | 2. they | 8. It |
| | 3. It doesn't | 9. It consists |
| | 4. they | 10. they |
| | 5. it is | 11. They are |
| | 6. them, they appreciate | 12. It is |

15·2 *Answers may vary.*
1. a few dishes
2. many airplanes
3. several animals
4. some students/coffee
5. a little argument/cotton
6. six meters
7. much courage
8. little kittens/rain

15·3
1. is
2. is
3. is
4. stays
5. was

| 15·4 | 1. much | 6. loaves |
|---|---|---|
| | 2. much | 7. a little |
| | 3. some | 8. the few |
| | 4. is | 9. much |
| | 5. much | 10. a little |

**15·5**
1. was
2. was
3. studies
4. wants
5. is
6. drinks

**15·6**
1. he OR she wants
2. they are
3. he OR she builds, his OR her
4. He, he OR She, she
5. he
6. his OR her OR their
7. his OR her OR their
8. he, his OR she, her OR they, their
9. it is
10. It is, It, it, his

**15·7** *Answers may vary.*
1. are
2. is
3. are
4. are
5. any
6. was
7. many

# 16 Using *other*

**16·1** *Answers may vary.*
1. another difficult task
2. another day at the office
3. another way of looking at things
4. another bowl of soup
5. other relatives of the bride
6. other kinds of problems
7. other goals of the project
8. other people to greet

**16·2**
1. the other
2. Others
3. another
4. others
5. The other
6. the other
7. Another, Another, Another, the other
8. Another, The other
9. the other
10. other
11. others
12. each other, one another, each other (OR ANY COMBINATION)
13. another
14. another
15. the other
16. the other
17. others, other people, others (OR ANY COMBINATION)
18. the others
19. other
20. another, Another, The other
21. Another, others
22. Another, The other
23. the others
24. another
25. each other OR one another
26. another
27. another

# 17 Gerunds

**17·1** *Answers may vary.*
1. drawing, practicing, sleeping late, juggling
2. hunting, kayaking, skiing, weightlifting

**17·2**
1. Moving
2. Mentioning
3. meeting
4. Managing
5. walking, swimming

**17·3**
1. reaching
2. Deciding
3. protecting, serving
4. studying, staying
5. painting, repairing
6. singing
7. alerting
8. Listening
9. Stretching
10. Rhyming, dancing

# 18 Conjunctions

**18·1** *Sample answers are provided.*
1. red, The car was small, dirty, and red.
2. muddy, The country lane was narrow, long, and muddy.
3. pollution, I dislike living downtown because of the noise, crime, and pollution.
4. kind people, The Dominican Republic has kind people, palm trees, pretty beaches, and tropical birds.
5. foods, I like to become acquainted with people, customs, and foods from other countries.

**18·2**
1. Susan washed the dishes and put the food away.
2. Peter opened the door and greeted the guests.
3. Ralph is painting the garage door and cleaning the brushes.
4. Simon is generous, handsome, and intelligent.
5. Please try to make less noise and have some respect for others.
6. She gave him chocolates on Monday, a CD on Tuesday, and a bracelet on Wednesday.
7. While we were in Los Angeles, we went to a concert, ate Mexican food, and visited old friends.
8. I should have finished my project and cleaned my car.
9. He preferred to play poker or spend time in museums.
10. I like water, but not soda.

**18·3**
1. and
2. so
3. but
4. or
5. but
6. nor
7. and
8. and

**18·4**
1. are
2. is
3. are
4. is
5. is
6. are

**18·5**
1. She has neither a pen nor a ruler.
2. Both the giant panda and the white tiger face extinction.
3. We could either drive or take the bus.
4. She wants to buy either a Honda or a Toyota.
5. We can either fix dinner for them at home or take them to the restaurant.
6. Not only Joseph but also Peter is absent. OR Both Joseph and Peter are absent.
7. Neither Joe nor Pedro is in class today.
8. You can have either tea or coffee.
9. Both Roger and Sam enjoy playing Nintendo.
10. The President's press secretary will neither confirm nor deny the story.
11. Both coal and petroleum are nonrenewable natural resources.
12. Both bird flu and malaria are dangerous diseases.
13. Neither her parents nor her boyfriend knows where she is.
14. According to the weather report, not only will it rain tomorrow but it will also be windy.

**18·6**
1. whether, or, for, and
2. and, either, or
3. not only, but, and
4. Neither, nor, but
5. Both, and, but

**18·7**
1. The men walked. The boys ran.
2. Sylvia came to the meeting. Her brother stayed home.
3. Sylvia came to the meeting, but her brother stayed home.
4. X
5. The professor spoke. The students listened.
6. His academic record was outstanding, yet he was not accepted into Harvard.
7. Her academic record was outstanding. She was not accepted into Harvard, but she was not too unhappy about it.
8. X
9. We had to go to the grocery store, for there was nothing to eat in the fridge.
10. A barometer measures air pressure. A thermometer measures temperature.
11. The Egyptians had good sculptors. Archeologists have found marvelous statues buried in the pyramids.
12. Murdock made many promises, but he had no intention of keeping them. He was known to be a liar.
13. I always enjoyed studying geography in high school, so I decided to pursue it in college.
14. Cecilia is in serious legal trouble, for she had no car insurance at the time of the accident.
15. Last night, Marie had to study for an exam, so she went to a coffeehouse.
16. The team of scientists has not finished analyzing the virus yet. Their work will not be published until later this year.
17. You have nothing to fear, for they are strong and united.
18. She threw the book out the window. She had failed the exam again, so she'd ruined her chances of bringing up her grade in the class.
19. Sophia struggled to keep her head above water. She tried to yell, but the water kept getting in her mouth.
20. The hurricane was devastating. Tall buildings crumbled and crashed to the ground.
21. It was a wonderful day at the park. The children swam in the river, collected rocks and insects, and laughed all day. The older kids played soccer. The adults prepared the food, supervised the children, and played cards for a short while.
22. Caterpillars eat plants and can cause damage to some crops, but adult butterflies feed primarily on flowers and do not cause any harm.
23. Both Jesse and I had many errands to do this morning. Jesse had to go to the post office and the bookstore. I had to go to the pharmacy, the video store, and the bank.
24. The butterfly is extraordinary. It begins as an ugly caterpillar and turns into something colorful. It almost looks like a piece of art.

**18·8**
1. although
2. before
3. until
4. because
5. before
6. while
7. since
8. even though
9. until
10. since OR because
11. because
12. when OR whenever
13. before OR when
14. if
15. than
16. after OR as soon as OR when
17. even though OR although
18. unless

**18·9**  *Sample answers are provided.*

1. They can't leave until they feed the cats.
2. I am not going to leave this room until you tell me the truth. OR Until you tell me the truth, I am not going to leave this room.
3. He can't pay his parking ticket until he receives his paycheck.
4. It had been a boring conversation until, finally, Steve arrived. OR Until Steve finally arrived, it had been a boring conversation.
5. When I go to bed at night, I like to read until I get sleepy.

**18·10**  *In these answers, the dependent clause beginning with* Now that *precedes the independent clause; however, it could also follow the independent clause.*

1. Now that Patrick moved into a house, he can use his own furniture.
2. Now that I've finally finished painting the kitchen, I can go running.
3. Now that it's winter, they have to wear warm clothes.
4. Now that he's 21, he can legally drink.
5. Now that Charles has a Jeep, he can drive to school.
6. Now that the civil war has ended, a new government is being formed.
7. Now that the project is finally over, we can relax.
8. Now that the water has gotten warmer, do you want to go swimming?
9. Now that my best friend is married, he has more responsibilities.
10. Now that I know English, I can get a job as a translator.

**18·11**  *Answers may vary.*

1. We stopped to visit our grandparents on our way to Oklahoma; afterwards/later/then, we stayed with friends in Tulsa.
2. We had planned to go to the park today; however/unfortunately, the rain canceled our plans.
3. It was a difficult time for her; still/however/nonetheless, she learned a lot from the experience.
4. The hotel stayed vacant and abandoned for many years; finally/eventually, the city council decided to tear it down.
5. They had a romantic walk along the river; afterwards/later, they went back to the hotel to drink some champagne.
6. Mr. Williams cannot speak at the conference; instead/therefore, Mr. Rogers will go in his place.
7. We enjoy all kinds of outdoor activities; for example, we really like rock climbing.
8. The mall is already closed; besides/anyway, you do not have any money to spend.
9. The essay must be written by Monday; otherwise, you fall behind schedule.
10. Anna Nicole Smith was incredibly rich; however, she did not have a happy life.
11. They spent their entire afternoon shopping for clothes; afterwards/later, they wore some of their purchases to the dance.
12. He likes seafood; however, he is allergic to oysters.

# 19 Prepositions

**19·1**
1. instead of, truck
2. in, pool; for, dinner
3. above, hills
4. about, book
5. into, room; next to, Helen
6. of, one
7. from, him; in, Iraq
8. Contrary to, opinion
9. among, students; from, department
10. with, table; by, window

**19·2**  *Answers may vary.*
1. her lovely garden
2. their sister
3. a chocolate éclair and a banana split
4. noon, sundown
5. the old monastery
6. the threat of a storm
7. your poor showing on the exam
8. the visitors to the museum
9. origami
10. the electrical storm

**19·3**
1. We spent a lot of time there.
2. They have been there for over three years.
3. In it, I found my sister's diary.
4. City Hall has been located here for years.
5. What are you hiding in them?
6. Do you really like its smell?
7. Their gowns looked like flour sacks.
8. His OR Her symphony was recently found.
9. They said her poems are their favorites.
10. Its political goals are slowly changing.

**19·4**  *Answers may vary.*
1. next to a school for the blind
2. beneath the first floor of a hotel
3. on the outskirts of Paris
4. of the state of Indiana
5. in the closet of his bedroom

# 20 Adjectives and adverbs

**20·1**
1. We had never arranged a surprise party for them.
   We had rarely arranged a surprise party for them.
2. The soprano from France never sang at the Met.
   The soprano from France rarely sang at the Met.
3. Grandfather was never in a good mood.
   Grandfather was rarely in a good mood.
4. My brother could never fix his own car.
   My brother could rarely fix his own car.
5. They will never go to Alaska in the winter.
   They will rarely go to Alaska in the winter.

**20·2**
1. hard
2. best
3. beautiful, happy
4. fast, good
5. humid
6. beaming, radiant
7. hurriedly
8. rarely
9. loudly
10. finally
11. often
12. biweekly
13. seriously
14. indoors
15. regularly
16. still
17. perhaps

**20·3**
1. meticulous, meticulously
2. easy, easily
3. loudly, loud
4. quietly
5. secretly
6. well, good

**20·4**
1. clean (*adj*), quite (*adv*), rapidly (*adv*)
2. Moroccan (*adj*), beautiful (*adj*)
3. old (*adj*), very (*adv*), carefully (*adv*)
4. usually (*adv*), rather (*adv*), short (*adj*)
5. very (*adv*), good (*adj*), yesterday (*adv*)

**20·5** *Answers may vary.*
1. Catherine has already finished writing the essay due tomorrow.
2. Helen is seldom at Jason's house.
3. Does he always go to her house?
4. He often goes hiking to get away from it all and relax.
5. She should always tell him the truth.
6. Eric has never seen the ocean.
7. Steven often produces his electronic music on his laptop.
8. Anna is often at the club on Tuesday nights.
9. Vince rarely goes to the movies, because he prefers staying home.
10. I generally don't ask for a girl's number if I don't know her.
11. I have never eaten an Asian pear.

# 21 Filler subjects and impersonal subjects

**21·1**
1. There was a cat sleeping under the coffee table.
2. There were several girls learning to dance ballet.
3. There will be a class photo taken at ten sharp.
4. There had been a lot of damage caused by the storm.
5. There are promises to be kept.

*Answers may vary.*
6. a violent storm last night
7. a meeting here recently
8. an important announcement in an hour
9. too many mistakes made
10. significant errors in your work

**21·2**
1. They
2. they, they
3. it
4. it
5. there
6. he
7. we OR they
8. it
9. it
10. it, it

**21·3** there, there, it, it, it, There, it

**21·4**
1. PP
2. IP
3. PP
4. IP
5. IP, IP

# 22 Clauses

**22·1**
1. she will be able to eat some dessert
2. Marco picked up something from the office
3. William read the cover story of *The Economist*
4. Barbara laughed
5. Paul watched
6. many people enjoy drinking a lot of it

**22·2**
1. The student that sits next to me is from Korea. OR The student, who sits next to me, is from Korea.
2. The boy that won first prize is excited. OR The boy, who won first prize, is excited.
3. I smelled the cake that was cooling on the window ledge. OR I smelled the cake, which was cooling on the window ledge.
4. We are studying English, which involves learning many rules.
5. We are studying sentences that contain different clauses.
6. I am using a relative clause that includes a possessive pronoun.
7. Physics problems require long calculations that are often very complex. OR Physics problems require long calculations, which are often very complex.
8. The bus driver that spoke to me a lot was friendly. OR The bus driver, who spoke to me a lot, was friendly.
9. I liked that girl that I met at the zoo last week. OR I liked that girl, whom I met at the zoo last week.
10. The movie that I saw was awful.
11. I liked the poem that he wrote.
12. His grandparents, whom we visited last month, were very nice.

**22·3**
1. I must thank your brother, from whom I received flowers. I must thank your brother, whom I received flowers from.
2. The woman with whom I spoke this morning was very kind. The woman that I spoke with this morning was very kind. The woman I spoke with this morning was very kind.
3. The conference that I registered for was interesting. The conference I registered for was interesting.
4. The painting, which I was looking at for a long time, was colorful and detailed. The painting that I was looking at for a long time was colorful and detailed. The painting I was looking at for a long time was colorful and detailed.
5. The man whom I was telling you about is sleeping over there. The man that I was telling you about is sleeping over there. The man I was telling you about is sleeping over there.

**22·4**
1. Mr. Castro, whose native language is Spanish, teaches a class for foreign students.
2. The yoga instructor whose class I am taking is excellent.
3. I met the man whose son is my office manager.
4. The woman whose apartment was on fire called 911.
5. I laughed at the man that I pushed in the pool.
6. I come from France, whose history goes back hundreds of years.
7. The people whose house we visited were crazy.
8. I sleep in a hotel whose residents are very noisy.
9. I have to call the girl whose cell phone I accidentally picked up after our date.
10. The boy, whose cheeks got sunburned while he was lying at the swimming pool, put lotion all over his face.

**22·5**
1. who put out the fire
2. I was waiting for
3. that she is wearing
4. Peter is working on
5. whose advice I take most seriously
6. I had last week
7. I was talking to
8. that destroyed the embassy

**22·6**
1. The younger men, whom we met in the hotel lobby this morning, are from Peru. The younger men that we met in the hotel lobby this morning are from Peru. The younger men we met in the hotel lobby this morning are from Peru.
2. I explained my absence to the manager, whose presentation I had missed. I explained my absence to the manager whose presentation I had missed.
3. Yesterday, I ran into Paul, whom I hadn't seen in months.
4. The driver, who was not paying attention, missed the red light.
5. He spoke of the postmodern movement, which I know nothing about. He spoke of the postmodern movement, about which I know nothing.
6. The historian, whom we met in Paris, is well known for his research. The historian that we met in Paris is well known for his research. The historian we met in Paris is well known for his research.
7. I am reading a novel that was written by Alexander Dumas.

8. The teacher, whom I questioned, gave good explanations. The teacher that I questioned gave good explanations. The teacher I questioned gave good explanations.
9. The professor, whose class I passed, gives easy exams.
10. I returned the car, which I had borrowed from my father. I returned the car that I had borrowed from my father. I returned the car I had borrowed from my father.
11. The hunter caught the lion, which had killed someone from the village. The hunter caught the lion that had killed someone from the village.
12. The children, whom I am taking care of, are very quiet. The children that I am taking care of are very quiet. The children I am taking care of are very quiet.

**22·7**
1. That is the cafeteria where I will eat lunch. OR That is the cafeteria that I will eat lunch in. OR That is the cafeteria I will eat lunch in.
2. The medieval village, where we spent our summer, was beautiful. OR The medieval village where we spent our summer was beautiful. OR The medieval village, in which we spent our summer, was beautiful. OR The medieval village, which we spent our summer in, was beautiful. OR The medieval village that we spent our summer in was beautiful. OR The medieval village we spent our summer in was beautiful.
3. The neighborhood where I grew up is dangerous. OR The neighborhood that I grew up in is dangerous. OR The neighborhood I grew up in is dangerous.
4. That is the account where I kept all my savings. OR That is the account that I kept all my savings in. OR That is the account I kept all my savings in.
5. Carl is from Jamaica, where I used to live.

**22·8** *Answers may vary.*
1. 1:10 P.M. is the time when my train arrives at the station.
2. June is the month when I will come.
3. 1959 is the year when the Cuban socialist revolution took place.
4. Wednesday is the day when my plane arrives.

**22·9**
1. That is the sidewalk where I parked.
2. That is the city where I was born.
3. That is the store where you do your grocery shopping.
4. That is the bank where you keep your money.
5. That is the building where he works.
6. That is the street where she lives.
7. That is the Mexican restaurant where we ate lunch.
8. That is the amphitheater where we have class.
9. That is the hotel where we spent our vacation.
10. That is the river where you went fishing.
11. That is the town where I lived until I was ten years old.
12. That is the university where your father went to graduate school.

**22·10**
1. Yes, the movie I watched was scary.
2. No, the iced coffee I drank did not taste good.
3. Yes, the scarf I bought keeps my neck warm.
4. No, the Chinese noodles I had for dinner were not too spicy.
5. Yes, the man I talked to answered my questions.
6. No, the little girl I saw was not wearing a pink sweater.
7. Yes, the football game I went to was exciting.
8. No, the bed-and-breakfast I stayed at was not in the countryside.
9. No, the exercise I am finishing is not difficult.
10. No, the letter I got in the mail was not from my aunt.

**22·11**
1. Neil Young is the musician whose album you are listening to.
2. Aline Helg is the professor whose class I am writing a thesis for.
3. Mr. Mohammed is the student whose notes I found.
4. Paul is an intern whose pen I borrowed.
5. The child whose ball you lost began to scream.
6. Your neighbors, whose house you stayed at, are very funny.
7. The executive, whose office is locked, has been in a meeting for five hours.
8. The woman whose necklace was stolen called a private detective.
9. Basquiat is the artist whose paintings you like the best.
10. Everyone tried to help the mother whose car had broken down.

**22·12** *Answers may vary.*
1. that he meets for the first time
2. who has the same birthday I do
3. who knows the answer
4. that I can do for her
5. that we can turn to
6. that he says is true
7. who hasn't sat down yet
8. that we took yesterday
9. who arrived late
10. who were in the first half, who were in the second half

**22·13**
1. Last night, the Metropolitan Movie Theater showed three of Stanley Kubrick's movies, one of which was *Dr. Strangelove*.
2. The village has three schools, two of which are high schools.
3. I tried on three hats, one of which I liked.
4. The capital has about five million people, the majority of whom are poor.
5. The army currently employs thousands of young men, all of whom have obtained their GED.
6. After the riots in Paris, over 400 people were arrested, many of whom were peaceful protesters.
7. They spread rumors about Catherine, one of whose faults was being beautiful beyond belief.

**22·14** *Answers may vary.*
1. which is really old
2. whom I had met last semester in Spanish class
3. whom live in Toulouse, France
4. which lasts only 35 minutes
5. whom I get along with
6. whose main problems is being disorganized
7. which were way too boring
8. which are being repainted

**22·15**
1. They bought an original Matisse painting, the value of which cannot possibly be estimated.
2. I bought a newspaper, the name of which is *Le Monde*.
3. We visited a Victorian castle, the interior of which was made of wood.
4. The United Nations is going through many changes, the outcome of which might alter human history.
5. My store's income is dependent on souvenirs, the sale of which depends on the number of tourists.

**22·16**
1. Clara was expelled from school, which took her family by surprise.
2. My husband never washes the dishes, which annoys me.
3. Pedro isn't home yet, which concerns me.
4. There was a fire in Key West, which means many villas burned.
5. I shut the car door on my finger, which was really silly of me.

**22·17** *Answers may vary.*
1. The person sitting behind us kept talking. The person sitting behind us kept talking, which distracted me a lot.
2. Alfred failed his math test. Alfred failed his math test, which shocked us all.
3. We got a call from the airport. We got a call from the airport, which means she'll be home anytime.
4. The food was freshly cooked. The food was freshly cooked, which I enjoyed very much.
5. They decided to sign the peace treaty. They decided to sign the peace treaty, which was unexpected good news.
6. The flight attendants kept snickering. The flight attendants kept snickering, which bothered me.
7. The neighbors' dog kept barking. The neighbors' dog kept barking, which annoyed me so much that I could not fall asleep.
8. My cousin was playing electric guitar. My cousin was playing electric guitar, which was so loud that it gave me a headache.

**22·18**
1. What she was mad about was important.
2. I don't know how well read she is.
3. Please tell me where you go shoe shopping.
4. I have no idea how old that child is.
5. Do you know whose pencil this is?
6. I don't know who those men are.

7. I can't tell who is coming to the meeting.
8. Let's ask her which flavor of ice cream she wants.
9. I can't recall how expensive it is.
10. I forgot what it is he sent me. OR I forgot what he sent me.
11. What she said to you is a lie!
12. Why she left the state is a mystery.
13. What we are doing at work is top secret.
14. What we are doing in English class today is easy.
15. Whom she is dating is none of your business.
16. I don't know who the president of Enron is.
17. I need to look up how old someone has to be in order to drink.

**22·19**
1. Why was George late for registration?
2. How long is it from San Antonio to the Mexican border?
3. What did Sarah sell?
4. Where does Pedro reside?
5. Who is that woman?
6. Whose computer is that?
7. Whom did Joseph see at the dinner?
8. Which movie does Sophie like best?
9. Who noticed Barbara at the bar?
10. When is the train scheduled to arrive?

**22·20**
1. why George was late for registration
2. how long it is from San Antonio to the Mexican border
3. what Sarah sold
4. where Pedro resides
5. who that woman is
6. whose computer that is
7. (the person) whom Joseph saw at the dinner
8. which movie Sophie likes best
9. who noticed Barbara at the bar
10. when the train is scheduled to arrive

**22·21**   *Answers may vary.*
1. I wonder where Adrian is.
2. I wonder who took the television remote.
3. I wonder whether you should call her.
4. I wonder whether Marie needs any help or not.
5. I wonder whether or not you left your keys on the counter.
6. I wonder who that man is.
7. I wonder what they are doing.
8. I wonder whether she is in trouble.
9. I wonder whether we should offer to help him.
10. I wonder whether we have enough time to go on vacation.
11. I wonder whose bike this is.
12. I wonder why the grass is so green.
13. I wonder how long a bonsai lives.
14. I wonder if there is life on Mars.
15. I wonder how the earth was created.

**22·22**
1. It is unfair that some immigrants don't receive equal pay for equal work. That some immigrants don't receive equal pay for equal work is unfair.
2. It is too bad that Patricia has not been able to make it to second grade. That Patricia has not been able to make it to second grade is too bad.
3. It is a well-known fact that alcohol abuse can ruin one's life. That alcohol abuse can ruin one's life is a well-known fact.
4. It is a fact that the sun is a star. That the sun is a star is a fact.
5. It is true that smoking can cause lung cancer. That smoking can cause lung cancer is true.
6. It is strange that Marc has made no friends here. That Marc has made no friends here is strange.
7. It is obvious that English is the principal language of the international business community. That English is the principal language of the international business community is obvious.

**22·23** *Answers may vary.*
1. to do
2. to wear
3. to move downtown or not
4. to play soccer
5. to get them
6. to eat, to visit certain exhibitions
7. to make lasagna, (to) make a Romano salad

**22·24**
1. Please let me know where to meet up with you.
2. The fireman told me how to stop a fire from spreading.
3. She told me when to get there.
4. Elizabeth liked both puppies, but she had trouble deciding which one to take home.
5. Alex played in a rock band that was successful, but Nathalie didn't know whether to buy their new album or not.

**22·25** *Answers may vary.*
1. take off his hat
2. forget about the whole case
3. be more honest with him
4. sing something for them
5. be as polite as possible from now on

# 23   Punctuation

**23·1**
1. The city council requested that Gov. Madison allocate more funds to the development of children's playgrounds.
2. Richard told his parents, "I enjoy having dinner before eight o'clock, because it gives me enough time to finish my homework before going to sleep."
3. Meet them at Whole Foods for breakfast.
4. Nathan said to his professor, "I can't be done with my paper by Monday."
5. I thanked Mrs. Bronco for giving us a ride to school this morning.
6. Sgt. Pepper was called to the conference room for an important membership meeting.

**23·2**
1. *The comma is used to separate the dependent clause from the main clause.*
2. *Commas are used to separate the elements of the address and to separate the date from the year.*
3. *The comma is used to separate the two independent clauses.*
4. *The comma is used to separate large numbers into smaller groups of digits.*
5. *The comma is used to separate the interrupting words as promised from the rest of the sentence.*
6. *The comma is used to separate the persons addressed from the rest of the sentence.*
7. *The comma is used to separate items in a series.*

**23·3**
1. Taylor asked, "How are we supposed to cook this with no oven?"
2. She packed two blouses, a black skirt, and a new business suit.
3. According to the U.S. Census Bureau, the world population reached 6,500,000,000 on February 25, 2006.
4. Dear Mrs. Dimple,
5. The Persian Gulf War officially ended on February 28, 1991.
6. They were so excited by the soccer game, which went into three overtimes, that they hardly noticed the afternoon go by.
7. Marie, Catherine, and Chris are all going to the theater together.
8. IBM, not Apple, will build a fast computer.
9. If you've never been to the craft show, there will be selected sales and bargain bins.
10. She will be participating, won't she?
11. Yes, I think there is enough time for you to pick it up and get back home before dinner.
12. If I could get a nickel for every time he lies, I would be a billionaire.
13. He had intended to stay home, but he decided instead to go running.

**23·4**

1. The computers at my job have large monitors, loud speakers, CD burners, DVD players, and all sorts of other useful hardware; are equipped with the most recent software; and have the most sophisticated firewall.
2. Peter was amazed by the talent of the opposing team's poetry skills; at the same time, he knew his team could win the poetry contest.
3. Greg was the first to run out of the burning house; however, Elizabeth was the one who made it to a pay phone to call the fire department.
4. Each of us had enough time to get in the hotel's swimming pool; nevertheless, we were all there on business.
5. There are moments when one needs to think about a situation calmly and for a long time; likewise, there are moments when one needs to make decisions quickly and instinctively.
6. Gina said, "Let's work as a group"; Peter said, "We should work individually instead"; and Andrew said, "Let's split the team, and while some can work as a group, others can work individually."
7. Karen has been painting the kitchen for three hours; all the while, she has been cooking and playing with the dogs.

**23·5**

1. She told me what her favorite colors were: blue, red, and light olive green.
2. Dear Madam President:
3. It is 5:30 A.M.; why are you calling me so early?
4. There are three main ingredients in a cake: sugar, flour, and eggs.
5. It was time for the lawyer to make his closing statement: "My client is an honest man, a hardworking man, a good husband, and he should not be sitting in this court today."
6. Nixon said: "Looting and pillaging have nothing to do with civil rights. Starting riots to protest unfair treatment by the state is not the best of solutions."
7. John has five trophies on his bookshelf: Four of them are from basketball tournaments.
8. The professor made an interesting statement during class: "We have not yet addressed the topic of social revolutions, which is a key component of our present argument."

**23·6**

1. Are you serious?
2. Get out of here now!
3. What do you think of the president's decision to go to war? his views on foreign policy? his thoughts on the economy?
4. Quickly! What are you waiting for?
5. Are you in a hurry?
6. When were you going to tell me?
7. Super!
8. That's so cool!
9. Do you think the corporation will apologize for unjustly firing those employees? taking away their retirement? not providing them with a severance package?
10. Are you out of your mind!

**23·7**

1. *The sentence refers to each person's painting methods, so 's is added to each name.*
2. Cassettes *is plural, not possessive, so it has no apostrophe.*
3. It's *has an apostrophe, because it is the contraction of* it is. Its walk *has no apostrophe, because* its *is possessive, referring to the dog's walk.*
4. The 1990s *is plural, not possessive, so it has no apostrophe.*
5. The Doors *is plural and possessive, so it has an apostrophe.*
6. *Because the two individuals own the car as a couple,* 's *is added to the second person's name only.*

**23·8**

1. The sergeant's boots were always the shiniest of all.
2. She really likes that about the '80s.
3. A doctor's quick intervention can save a life.
4. There are times when the UN's presence has prevented armed conflict.
5. Who's winning today?
6. X
7. X
8. Natalie's new bicycle is red and yellow.
9. The Cutlips' cat wandered into our garage this morning.
10. Her mother's and father's wills were drafted by the lawyer.

**23·9**
1. I met a woman who said she could make "magic potions."
2. From what I hear, Joseph said the turning point in the novel is when Carlito tells his cousin, "You should have never worked with Francisco in the first place; he's not to be trusted."
3. She read "The Palm-Tree" and was very moved by the poem.
4. What do you think of John Coltrane's tune "My Favorite Things"?
5. The morning newspaper mentioned that there might be "snow tonight with a chance of hail and strong winds."
6. His father asked him, "What would you like to do this summer, work or travel?"
7. As Patrick walked away, she hesitated and then screamed, "Will you go out with me?"
8. X (*Book titles are italicized.*)
9. We analyzed the play *The Flies* by Jean-Paul Sartre and his famous essay "Americans and Their Myths." (*Titles of plays are italicized.*)
10. The song "Organ Donor" is best qualified as "groundbreaking."
11. The photographer encouraged the model by telling her, "You're doing really well, but I want you to relax a little more. When the camera is pointed at you, just imagine someone is saying to you, 'You're the only one that can do this,' and I want you to believe it!"

**23·10**
1. Eric could not figure out how to get out of the maze—how silly and useless he felt!
2. The touchdown scored by the Patriots was an 83-yard play.
3. They were once considered wishy-washy.
4. Carla was about to close the front door and thought to herself—do I have everything I need in the bag?
5. The tight-lipped receptionist told the reporters nothing.
6. She detests animal testing, so she never buys Yves Saint-Laurent products.
7. Thirty-two of the 52 figure skaters missed at least one of their jumps.
8. The Security Council voted against three crucial resolutions—an armed attack, a forced embargo, and unified retaliation.

**23·11**
1. *The Skibby Chronicle* [published anonymously in the 1530s but now believed to be the work of Poul Helgesen] describes Danish history from 1047 to 1534.
2. As members of the book club, we had to read *The Stranger* (Albert Camus [1913–1960]) and discuss the novelist's concept of the absurd.
3. According to historical accounts, the first bridge over the Chattahoochee River there [Columbus, Georgia] was built by John Godwin in 1832–33.
4. They were told there was a heavy load of work that they would have to deal with during the semester: They would have to (1) take two three-hour exams, (2) read 13 books, and (3) write a 50-page essay.
5. Thomas Hart Benton (1888–1975) finished his famous *Indiana Murals* in 1932.
6. Some scholars argue that Michelangelo (noted Italian painter and inventor [1475–1564]) was the quintessential Renaissance man.

# 24 Capitalization, numbers, and italics

**24·1**
1. Teresa Malcolm is president of the Ford Rotary Club.
2. In three weeks, we will be traveling through France, Switzerland, and Spain.
3. The night sky was so clear we could see the entire moon, Venus, and Jupiter.
4. As soon as he got home, Patrick felt like putting on his new Adidas swimsuit.
5. The Second World War lasted nearly six years.
6. The novel we bought at the airport was *The Da Vinci Code.*
7. I visited the Empire State Building when I was in New York.
8. Thelma and John saw the launch of the *USS Enterprise.*
9. The NAACP is a prominent organization based in the United States.
10. They told her, "We don't like the proposal you've written."

**24·2**
1. Marilyn is the president of the Ladies of Grace at her church.
2. Some restaurants in Los Angeles serve Americanized European food.
3. Members of all faiths gathered on campus to protest, including Christians, Jews, Muslims, and Hindus.
4. "The Red Wheelbarrow" by William Carlos Williams is one of the most profound poems I've read.

5. They came from the Eastern states in search of gold.
6. We read *Of Mice and Men* last week for class.
7. The CIA agent said he often works with FBI investigators, as well as with representatives of the FAA.
8. A speaker from the National Transportation Safety Board gave a presentation on the most common accidents that took place on Interstate 66.

**24·3**
1. An important date to remember is November 17, 1959.
2. The city paid $34.7 million to build the tower.
3. It took five out of nine members to reach a consensus.
4. In Europe, the 1970s were marked by social and political change.
5. Turn to page 109, which should be chapter 12.
6. The morning temperature was 47 degrees Fahrenheit, or 8 degrees Celsius.
7. X
8. They drove down Interstate 34 to the lake.
9. The Second Battle of Bull Run was fought from August 28 to 30, 1862.

**24·4**
1. We installed *Windows Vista* on our desktop today.
2. Jason's Spanish literature class read Miguel de Cervantes' *Don Quixote*.
3. They reviewed the case of *The People v. Robert Page Anderson* for their law class.
4. He invited 10 of his closest friends, but more than 90 people showed up.
5. Did you get a copy of the *Atlantic Monthly*?
6. The lawyer working on *Miller v. Wilson* offered his services *pro bono*.
7. The Baton Rouge *Advocate* gave us information about visiting the Garden District.
8. The detective speculated about the criminal's *modus operandi*.

# Appendix   Review exercises

**A·1**
1. have to
2. has to be able to
3. is able to
4. should be
5. had better
6. am going to have to
7. am going to
8. had better be able to

**A·2**
1. Have you met, have ever had
2. are you doing, am trying, is jamming, be putting OR put, will probably hurt
3. is sitting, see, certainly looks
4. is, was running, came, fell, don't, Are, were, seems, be suffering
5. Are you taking, am not, Have you ever taken, have, did you take, taught OR was teaching, am taking, Is, was taking OR took, was, was
6. spent, had never been, did you do, drove, thought
7. has been, rained, dropped, is, was shining, changes, knows, am, will have frozen
8. went, Was it, didn't, enjoyed, did you see, had never seen, saw, went, thought, was, didn't

**A·3**
1. is [going]
2. should [open]
3. is [going]
4. don't have to [paint]
5. Are supposed to [get]
6. should have to [pay]
7. is going to [open]
8. have been [running]
9. should be able to [stay]
10. has been [playing]

**A·4**
1. Kenji has been studying Portuguese. OR Kenji is studying Portuguese.
2. Juan has lived in Madrid for two years.
3. He has to come back to meet us here.
4. My father, Raoul, who studied mathematics with my uncle, is looking for a job.
5. After work, Anjali will be going to the pub. OR After work, Anjali will go to the pub.
6. Last week, Mark was able to visit the president's office.
7. The soil is dry. They will not be able to plant vegetables there.
8. He doesn't like his neighbors, because they're too noisy.
9. They didn't have any problems with the rental car.
10. I have been learning a lot since I began doing my exercises.
11. Are you thinking of buying another car soon?
12. She was visiting many monuments when she was in Rome. OR She visited many monuments when she was in Rome.
13. I didn't see a single beautiful sunset.
14. He couldn't forget her after the love affair.
15. He is always attempting to catch the students cheating. OR He was always attempting to catch the students cheating.
16. Sometimes when I cross the street, I don't look to see if a car is coming.
17. I've been thinking about it for a long time now. OR I've thought about it for a long time now.
18. I feel my English grammar might be improving. OR I feel my English grammar might improve.
19. Mrs. Gilmore was sad, because her son had to go back to the front lines.
20. All my friends can help me become a better person.

**A·5**
1. painters
2. classes
3. X
4. laws
5. workers
6. societies
7. customs

**A·6**
1. be
2. be OR have been
3. have
4. had
5. have
6. did
7. have
8. is

**A·7**    *Answers may vary.*
1. *This is a sentence fragment or a dependent clause:* Teaching math to smart students is interesting. OR I love teaching math to smart students.
2. X (*Listen! is an imperative.*)
3. *This is a sentence fragment or a dependent clause:* If you want to observe what is taking place, you should stand up.
4. X
5. *This is a sentence fragment:* The European Union is composed of many different countries.
6. *This sentence needs a period at the end:* I already ran three miles.
7. *The first word of this sentence needs to begin with a capital letter:* Before I walked in, I rang the bell, hoping someone would open the door.
8. *This is a sentence fragment:* There are many different photographs in that dusty, black book.
9. *This is a sentence fragment:* Peter has many children.
10. X (*Open is an imperative.*)
11. X
12. X
13. *The main clause of this sentence is missing a subject:* If your friend is a lawyer, he doesn't have to worry about finding a job.
14. *This sentence has redundant subjects:* Madrid is the capital of Spain. OR It is the capital of Spain.
15. *This sentence is missing a verb:* Also, he is very smart, quiet, and polite.

**A·8**   *Answers may vary.*

1. When I was younger, I thought the earth was flat.
2. X
3. My favorite color was red, because it reminded me of my sister.
4. He hates horror movies because he gets scared immediately.
5. X
6. She is back: It's the end of spring semester at UCLA.
7. To paint this wall, you need a special brush.
8. Elvis is over there with Tupac and Biggie, and they look happy.
9. You will get a free subscription. In addition, you will receive a free towel, a matching bathrobe, a sticker, and a silver pen.
10. Once you have done all your stretching, run for two miles or so.
11. X
12. When the water is boiling, put the pasta in the pot.
13. After the sun comes up, we can begin hiking up the mountain.

**A·9**

1. be promoted
2. give
3. knock
4. be
5. have
6. be studied, (be) stopped
7. be allowed
8. be postponed
9. remain
10. be named
11. take
12. write
13. meet
14. talk
15. join
16. be
17. be admitted
18. not be
19. return
20. not tell

**A·10**

1. The private and public sectors in Africa need to work closely together.
2. It is undeniable that armed conflict makes things worse.
3. They sit on the bench and feel that the judge condemns them for no apparent reason.
4. Many families in this area who don't own houses feel that they should get interest-free loans.

**A·11**

1. is worn
2. was invented
3. spelled
4. will be built
5. is scheduled
6. was confused
7. were frightened
8. was offered
9. was expected
10. was reported
11. was killed OR had been killed
12. was ordered
13. was caused
14. will be divided

A·12    1. When we get older, we can do a lot of things.
    2. Pedro ate a few pieces of cheese with his enchilada.
    3. He read some books at the public library before they closed.
    4. Last year, I gave him *Star Wars* and *Indiana Jones* for Christmas, but I don't know if he ever watched those movies.
    5. There are too many people in this car.
    6. My little sister is only three years old, but she seems older.
    7. We had not been to Portugal in six years.
    8. X
    9. If you want to form your own opinion, you should read many news articles and watch many kinds of documentaries.
   10. In addition to the art gallery, there are a lot of beautiful places to visit.

A·13    1. She will be going to Dallas to visit her brother.
    2. Patrick has known me since I was six years old.
    3. He has been living in Lisbon for years, but we still keep in touch via e-mail.
    4. When I get to Peter's house, he will have to open the front door.
    5. I soon noticed that Paul didn't drive very well. Among other things, he didn't respect the speed limit on the highways.
    6. Paul knows that he should be taking driving classes.
    7. If he were to move back home, he could help his mom more and he could take care of her on a daily basis.
    8. Vanessa should do her shopping at Trader Joe's.
    9. I am taking the GRE next month, and I am quite nervous.

A·14    1. In terms of transportation, cars are a basic part of modern life.
    2. The automobile has made it possible for people to travel many miles from their homes.
    3. X
    4. Students study more than they used to and learn about more things than they used to.
    5. Life expectancy is much greater than it was a hundred years ago.

A·15    1. The ten districts in this city have decided to build more modern-looking buildings.
    2. Some cities in Argentina surprise tourists with their architecture.
    3. Often, the term "third-world country" makes people think of crime and poverty.
    4. X
    5. The graduate courses are very difficult; you feel like everyone else understands and you don't.
    6. Study a lot, and you will get many of the answers right.
    7. If a student doesn't understand the answer to his or her question, he or she should feel comfortable enough to ask again.
    8. All students have to take the two parts of the exam.
    9. These drills cannot prove the ability of the nurses, because the nurses simply execute certain emergency procedures.
   10. There are two kinds of people in this company: honest people and greedy people.
   11. There are many problems at my office, but one problem is the lack of motivation.
   12. Any person whose parents are seriously sick worries about their health.
   13. You can find many kinds of people working in our office.
   14. Italian ice cream is so delicious. I'm pretty sure you'll like it.
   15. When I first came to this hotel, I didn't like the food, but now I like it very much.
   16. That was the first time I bought my own furniture. I enjoyed picking it out, and I felt like an adult.
   17. The people who share my apartment are friendly, but they're messy.
   18. There are six freshly planted trees on my street.
   19. If you drive when you're too tired, you might cause an accident.
   20. I left my wallet and my keys on the counter. When I came back, I couldn't find them anymore.
   21. Everyone wants to be successful and be in good health.
   22. Count the money again before you put it in the envelope.
   23. Every person should help improve his or her neighborhood.

A·16    1. X
    2. Christine enjoys walking along the river. She likes that it's so peaceful.
    3. My boyfriend's mother is an attorney. She works for important people.
    4. X
    5. He needed a coffee table and a couch, but he decided he could live without them.
    6. My cousins are all younger than I, but they are taller than I am.

7. Japan is a small country. It has a long history.
8. Many people in the world are learning English. These people want to improve their language skills and get better jobs.
9. If the tourists go to Puerto Rico, they should visit Old San Juan. They ought to try the food, too, because it's delicious.
10. All his ideas come from dreams, and he tries to make these dreams reality.
11. Mrs. Hutchinson put her jacket back on.

**A·17**
1. This government has been run by Cardinal Richelieu since 1626.
2. I'm quite excited to see her again.
3. I am so happy. Finally, I passed the exam.
4. They're not sure if the problem will be worked out by tomorrow.
5. I'm interested in advanced technology.
6. The other colors have to be changed.
7. We need to love someone and be loved.
8. This question can be decided by taking into account all the information we've gathered.
9. I like the people there, because they're very educated.
10. I like the way math is taught in her class.
11. This store is located on the third floor of the mall.

**A·18**
1. was offered
2. was held up, took
3. is spent
4. was not admitted, had already begun
5. were working, occurred
6. generally delivers
7. will be used
8. was studying, is finally getting OR has been studying, has finally gotten
9. are being sold
10. will never be forgotten
11. arrive, will be met, will be wearing, will be standing
12. has been OR was, lost, dropped, was walking, broke, was stolen

**A·19**
1. is produced
2. saw, was interviewed
3. are controlled, are determined
4. blew, cost
5. is being treated
6. is exposed, affects
7. was poisoned
8. is supported
9. was told
10. will probably be lost
11. were sent
12. will be developed, have already been tested